MEN'S OPTIMISATION BIBLE

To my younger self, who needed this book
more than you could possibly know.

Introduction

If you have purchased this book, it is likely because you have decided to take responsibility for improving your life... to unlock who it is that you are & where it is you want to go.
It is because you are ready to begin carving out a path for your future.
Them momentary flickers of motivation you feel before the dismal return to reality... they are soon to be a relic of the past.

Over the course of our time together you will gradually eliminate procrastination of a future full of peace, harmony & 'success' – whatever that means for you. In doing so, you will begin to understand what it is that you truly desire from life. We will take aim from here, both in the realm of the physical & the metaphysical.
This book is designed to inspire change.
Now is not the time to outsource your fate or cry victim to the outside world. No... now is where the work begins!

What you are about to read, I believe, are some of the most important principles you need to create a positive movement forward in your life & to become the optimal version of yourself.
It is my most sincere hope that, upon completion of this book, you are able to establish the attitudes, beliefs & behaviours required to bring forward the best version of yourself into the world.

Throughout this book I have made my best effort to address all areas of life that I feel can produce a positive, healthy, masculine view for your future. Penetrating both the external & internal environment, we will delve into every aspect of life that can, if worked on with discipline & diligence, bring forth the best 'you' possible.

Many of us feel lost in our current society – a society that has a distinct lack of adequate male role models & a misguided, dare I say twisted, view of masculinity. Despite addressing society at large, the main premise of this book is to turn the spotlight onto what you can control... <u>You</u>.

There is little new here. Whilst I have applied my own touch in areas, this book would be nothing without the incredible philosophers, psychologists & other professionals, experts & modern-day influencers whose knowledge & expertise is referenced throughout.

It would be disingenuous for me not to recognize their astounding influence over this book & equally over my own thinking & writing.

This book includes data from scientific research & traditional books, as well as broadening into modern forms of data collection such as interviews, podcasts & even, at times, social media. In doing this, it has allowed for a greater array of data collection, uniquely applied from one chapter to the next.

I in no way proclaim that what is written in this book is indisputable fact, & as such, I am open to any critique or amendment.

Throughout this book, I am simply acting as a messenger. Not in some messianic way but, rather as a lay person, as a member of the public just like you, who has grown increasingly concerned with the cultural discussion around masculinity & the detrimental downstream effects that are becoming all too prevalent in our culture as a result.

Despite having made my best attempts to credit the individuals' whose work & knowledge I have been fortunate enough to access over the last few years in the process of writing this book, I am only human & I am only too aware of my own shortcomings. Therefore, if I have misquoted an individual or have failed to attribute a credit or citation where appropriate, please feel free to reach out & allow me to make the necessary amendment. Some of the references & citations may be ever so slightly misquoted due to their source format (such as podcasts where an accurate transcript was not present). In these cases, I have endeavoured to relay the quote as precisely as possible, though there may be some punctuation & formatting errors within.

Some of what you are about to read may sound contradictory. For example, some chapters will talk of suffering & failure, & becoming accustomed to the hardships of life... it will speak to working hard & overcoming the odds.
Other areas of the book will address the underlying beliefs that can sometimes fuel such endeavours & how these can be damaging, as opposed to liberating.

It will talk about excelling in your chosen field, then go on to address the maintenance of healthy relationships & a sense of self-worth outside of this one specific area of your life.

Contradictory though it may seem, I have my reasons for this, as detailed below.

Firstly, it is because all the chapters in this book have relevance to men. Whilst some chapters may resonate more than others, if I were to speak only of health (physical & mental) it would fail to address many other facets of life that are equally as important.

Further, if I spoke purely of masculinity & the strength required to be a stable, competent, desirable man, but failed to address the areas of life that required introspection & nurturing (be that internally or externally) you would not gain the depth of understanding that is required to bring a fully-formed version of yourself forward; whether that be in your relationships, social interactions, at work, or in the way you treat yourself.

In addition to this, one individual may be a high achieving, 'type A', industrious individual &, as such, find the chapter on 'Stress' (& the mitigation of said stress) of particular interest. Yet, another man may have been brutally emasculated in his maturation period & conditioned to be 'more like girls' (not uncommon in today's era) &, for this man, he may find the chapter on 'Responsibility' or 'Masculinity' of particular importance.

There are many iterations of this & it is my hope that the book has laid out something for every man to benefit from. To put it simply, if I think it is important information, it is in this book.

What you do (or don't do) matters.
It affects you. It affects others. It affects the world.
We can change for better or for worse… take the decision to choose the former over the latter by turning the page & committing to your future.

Let's do this!

DISCLAIMER:

CONTENTS:

Identity

Who are you?
No, not the song... Who are *you*?

Let us begin by developing a greater understanding of
what it is that makes you, you.
What are the things that constitute your identity?
Take some paper & a pen. Place 'you' in the middle of the
page. Now give yourself some room to expand out all of
the segments of what makes you, you. This used to be
referred to as a 'mind-map', though it is entirely possible
that by now some ideologue has found a reason to claim
it to be an offensive term. Either way, extend out in each
direction with the different aspects that constitute your
identity. Then branch out further on each aspect if
applicable.

I will provide a basic example below:

This is a very rudimentary demonstration. Nevertheless, it provides the basic outline from which you can develop your own mind-map. Branch off from each characteristic with the personality traits (if you are aware of them, i.e. creativity, introversion/extroversion etc) & what each aspect reveals to you about yourself.

Give yourself space & time here. Introspect as if you are thoroughly investigating yourself. Keep penetrating on each area until you have exhausted all aspects.
This may open your eyes to aspects of your personality that you were unaware of. It may show you that, currently, there isn't much that constitutes who you are. We do not all have the same starting point here & it is important to realise exactly that; this is the *starting* point. If nothing else, this exercise will have given you the conscious awareness of what constitutes your identity.

So, how many things did you have?
Are you a sportsman? If so, what sport? What role do you play? What are the characteristics of that role?
Are you a businessman? An entrepreneur? What personality traits does that role embody? Where do you excel? Where do you fall short?
Would your findings align with how your friends would describe you?
Ruminate on this point for a while. Make any necessary adjustments or points of reflection. Perhaps you can see some discrepancies in how you see yourself, verses how you are actually behaving.

The things that constitute our identity will change overtime. Perhaps you will bear witness to this across the duration of this book.

Your character forms over infinite repetitions. Our identity is, quite literally, what we do repeatedly. This may be daunting to comprehend. Yet it can be revitalising to know that, if you aren't currently where you want to be, or are not *who* you want to be, this <u>can</u> change.

It is my hope that upon completion of this book, you will also know how to enact such a change.

More often than not, we fail to paint an accurate picture of ourselves. We are ignorant of our shortcomings. Perhaps they are too painful to acknowledge. We indulge in our own narcissistic self-interest, operating through our subconscious motivations & running a preordained script from our childhood.

Unbeknown to us, the people that exist in our immediate vicinity are sometimes able to pick up on this. They are not tainted by our own delusions of ourselves. This is why there may exist a differential between your own concept of self & that which is perceived by the outside world.

It must be noted that every human has an inbuilt capacity for narcissism. Each of us will have felt that, at least at one point in our lives, we were the centre of attention. We all have an ego &, as a social species, we love to have that ego stroked by others.

It is important to understand this inbuilt narcissism we each hold because it is equally prevalent in those we meet. That angelic glow you see yourself in, that spotlight that seems to only shine on you, every other person sees that manifest in themselves.

Some individuals possess a level of narcissism that can be deeply manipulative & damaging, yet most of us have it under control insofar that it does not intrude upon our lives, or the lives of others, in an unhealthy way. It is important to become aware that we all hold this capacity. We all have a yearning to be accepted & to be valued. We want to feel important.

There is, however, a way for us to establish a positive self-image… one that is mirrored back to us through the way we show up in society.

A lot of our identity formulates in our early childhood. We are understandably ignorant of how we are being continuously shaped by our environment. As children we are born with different temperaments, seek out different activities & steadily develop into young adults with certain skills & interests. It is often encouraged that children try a variety of activities & subject areas so as to develop both cognitively & socially. Despite this, many of us will have found a particular interest in childhood that took dominance.

If, when answering the above questions, there were many different aspects to your identity, that will very likely be advantageous to your psychological wellbeing. Having a unidimensional identity leaves no room to manoeuvre in times of change & uncertainty… & life is full of uncertainty!

What happens if your identity is wrapped in being an athlete, but you get a catastrophic injury & cannot compete? Or when you inevitably reach the age at which you are past peak performance? What happens to who you are when you enter the next stage of your life, when your current pursuit is no longer necessary, or even possible?

Many of our goals & pursuits (which shape our identity) can be quite arbitrary. If your goal is to gain muscle, why is it not to lose fat? If you aspire to become CEO of your company, why not start your own company? If your goal is to save £100,000, why not £200,000?
It is important to pay attention to your decisions & be specific with what you want from your life & why. Is this what *you* want or has it been thrust upon you from an outside influence, consciously or otherwise?

Our culture will influence our decisions, as will our family & our friendship group. Only you will know if you are speaking & acting out *your* truth. To find that out you must ask yourself & you must want to know the answer. This can be very de-stabilizing as questions of this nature make the chaos of life manifest in our conscious awareness. That is a very unsettling feeling. There is no light without dark &, as you will read throughout this book, it is only by taking the journey inside that we can embody who we truly are in this world.
As the famous psychologist Carl Jung said, "*unless you make the unconscious conscious, it will direct your life and you will call it fate*".

In the current left-leaning, liberal society we find ourselves living in the West, we would scold at the term 'discrimination'. Yet, each of us discriminate with every decision we make.

In order to pursue one goal, you must rule out the pursuit of another. To commit to one monogamous partner, you have to say no to all other potential partners. To pursue a career within the company you work for you have to rule out all other industries, then you have to rule out every other company within that industry. In order to progress in said company, you may even have to rule out other aspects of your life (most highly successful businessmen have to possess insane levels of conscientiousness & stress tolerance whilst simultaneously working >60 hours per week... *there's not much room for a work/life balance*).

What do you want to do with your life?

Many people today struggle to know what it is they want to do with their life. You could argue that this has always been the case, only that in the modern/digital age there is so much choice that many of us fall into paralysis by analysis. There is always something better on the horizon. Some hot new job comes up or a new industry or a quick way to make money online. The world is changing rapidly & people don't know where to, nor do they necessarily want to, invest their time & money for their future.

This is likely to be magnified with the introduction of artificial intelligence. We have no idea how much disruption will be caused through the implementation of AI, which we are clearly on the precipice of now. Furthermore, many young adults do not know what they want to do as they have begrudgingly completed the school system, been (en)rolled through college & all the while have never been taught to think about what they are interested in &/or can make a viable income from in the future.

Let's address this now:
Grab a piece of paper & on one side write down all of the things that you enjoy in life – anything from the smallest pleasure of making a cup of coffee in the morning or waking up without your dreaded alarm clock, all the way through to achieving a personal best in the gym, taking a luxury vacation, getting a promotion at work or having sex.
On the other side of the paper, write down all of the things that are unsatisfying & leave you feeling frustrated or lethargic. Again, include all of the things that create a slight moment of unease or irritation, right the way through to the things that make you physically enraged & violently angry.

The point of this activity is not to assess which things are within our control & which are not (*addressed later in the chapter 'Stoicism in the Postmodern Age'*). Nor is it to speak to our value hierarchy & whether we are orchestrating ourselves toward a meaningful & purposeful life (*addressed later in the chapters 'Purpose & Responsibility' & 'Value hierarchies, Habits &*

Behaviour change'). The purpose is to open our eyes to who we are, what it is that we like & dislike &, finally, to see if we are living a life that is bringing us a sense of joy & fulfilment. It's amazing how many of us live on autopilot, never taking control of our life. Hopefully you have now generated a clearer idea of what you truly like & dislike whilst mitigating (as best you can) any external influence.

Keep this list & add to it overtime. You'll be surprised at how many things can bring you moments of pleasure & joy, as well as how many things lower your mood & drain your energy. As stated earlier, if nothing else this will bring you to a greater understanding of yourself.

You have a limited amount of time here, one day you will be old & you will no longer have the energy or the resources to make a change or to start something new. There is only so much you can do. There is only so much time in any given day. Cast aside the things that you find sucking the joy from your life & find time to be present doing the things that you enjoy & that give you purpose.

Regarding work & employment, it is perhaps more effective to look at what actions you enjoy doing, as opposed to what job/career you want. If your dream job entails daily actions & behaviours that you do not enjoy, the likelihood of that 'dream job' being truly fulfilling for you is very low.

Chasing money can also be problematic. The most well-paid job is not necessarily the job 'you' want.

Take a moment to think about the following question, "why is it that you do what you do?"

It goes without saying that the game of money is a particularly difficult one to manage & I do not want to sound be condescending here.

We exist in a period of time that is unprecedented. The growth of the middle class has been an enormous cultural phenomenon in recent generations. We often take it for granted today that we have gas, water & electricity at a constant & that we have TV, entertainment & utilities in the home that make our quality of life more comfortable than ever before.

The obvious caveat here is that not everyone has an equal share of the spoils. Some people struggle more than others to make ends meet. This is a problem that is inevitable in society, just as it is in nature.

No matter how egalitarian you make a society there will always be inequality in virtually every metric. This appears to be a fundamental truth of existence, no matter what controls are enforced. Equality simply isn't in natures' interest. This shows us how incredible it is that we have been able to establish a system of democracy within our civilisation, in spite of the inevitable inequality present in all things.

Many left-leaning individuals in our society may bellow the rhetoric of equality for all which, on the surface, seems honourable. Yet it is important to see through this saintly exterior to understand these beliefs for what they truly are, a play for power.

There is no such thing as complete equality, no matter how much this is pushed.

Now for the condescending bit!

Money will fill your pockets, but passion & purpose fill the soul. There are many rich millionaires who are desperately lonely & depressed. You may be cynical & say "well they're depressed but at least they have tons of money". You think you wouldn't have that problem, of course. To which I would say, firstly you know nothing about them. Further, you know little about human beings if you think money is the thing that should make you happy regardless of anything else. Lastly, I'd say you probably don't know yourself too well &, even if you do, you likely have no idea how you would respond if you were in that position.

Nevertheless, if you are aiming to conquer the game of money it would be advisable to focus on *what* you are doing & *who* you are doing it with, rather than focusing simply on how *hard* you are working. That hard work is wasted if you choose the wrong game to play.

Some of the hardest workers in the world live at or under subsistence level. Why? Because they didn't choose the correct game to play. Take, for example, labourers, construction workers or bricklayers.

*I must caveat this point as many of these tradesmen, listed above, earn very well &/or have chosen this specific field intentionally. In fact, with the AI revolution/4th Industrial Revolution imminent, & the subsequent potential of many high-paying white-collar jobs disappearing, these career paths could very well be favourable & advantageous today!

What type of job/career would suit you?

Evidently, we live in a specialist society. However, each of us have been socialized through the institution of the school system to be a good generalist – to be above average in a variety of areas. You can see a contradiction there. You know nothing about economics & leave school conditioned to enter a position of wage labour within society. Little thought if any is given to becoming an entrepreneur or a business owner. In fact, any aspiration outside of the world of wage labour is typically beaten out of us by our current, outdated school model; one that is based on top-down authority & blind obedience, bleeding over from the factory era of the Industrial Revolution.

Unfortunately, it is in the areas that are *not* taught in the school system that a) keep the infrastructure of society running & b) scale financially. These skills are generally found in manual work; trades, utilities, engineering, computing etc, or through entrepreneurship.
Therefore, as you enter the workplace you have no idea how society works or where you need to position yourself to be successful. Until this changes, perhaps the only thing to do is to taste different jobs, experiment with different sectors & see where you may be best suited. Search for what job role & employment type provides you with the best fit.

What you have just read may appear contradictory in relation to the above statement of choosing the wrong

'game' to play. There are jobs in most industries that scale financially & there are others that do not. For example, if the inputs are closely tied to the outputs, it will not scale as well as a job where the inputs & outputs are disproportionately related to one another. Most financial success, aside from choosing a field that is integral to the workings of society, comes from leverage. As noted earlier, our Western school system produces workers. Workers have little to no leverage.
It is unlikely that you will become rich by renting out your time.

All of this assumes being rich is the answer. Let it be made clear; it is not. Money can solve your money problems, but that's where it ends. How long do you think you will be able to turn up consistently to a job you hate?
This is by no means a recommendation to throw away your job if you have nothing else lined up. It is the mere suggestion that perhaps you could aim to find something that is more aligned with who you are, thus eliminating the resistance to work.

"Specific knowledge is found by pursuing your genuine curiosity and passion rather than whatever is hot right now…
Building specific knowledge will feel like play to you but will look like work to others" (1).

An effective means of understanding where you may be best positioned to maximise your potential would be to take the time to rigorously contemplate where you are positioned on the spectrum of the 'Big 5' personality traits. Where do you sit in terms of your capacity for Openness, Conscientiousness, Extroversion, Agreeableness, Neuroticism?

This is not a recommendation to undertake some random personality test. Most personality tests lack the scientific underpinnings & replicability necessary for the results to be applicable to your life (2). For example, McCarley & Carskadon (1983) report only 47% of their respondents retained their initial types over a period of 5 weeks (3). Further, the National Research Council determined that MBTI should not be used in career counselling until supported by research (4).

A process such as 'self-authoring' would give you a far more robust picture of who you are & where you could position yourself in the world. This can then provide you with an understanding of what jobs may be better suited to you & how you can bring forth the best version of yourself into the world.

"People who spend time writing carefully about themselves become happier, less anxious and depressed and physically better. They become more productive, persistent and engaged in life". That extract was taken from the 'self authoring suite', established by Jordan B. Peterson, Daniel M. Higgins, & Robert O. Pihl (5).

Obviously, you need to have the prerequisite intelligence (IQ/grades) & the ability to do a particular job but, with that accounted for, long term success in a chosen field will be largely influenced by where your personality sits across the 'Big 5' – as well as some other advantages such as having a high stress tolerance. As stated by Jordan Peterson in a University lecture titled, 'Personality 18: Biology & Traits (published on YouTube in 2017); "*almost all jobs that are at the top of complex dominance hierarchies require very high intelligence & insane levels of conscientiousness... as well, generally speaking, as pretty damn high levels of stress tolerance*" (6).

Finding a job that is suited for you (think Big 5 personality traits) is undoubtedly important for your general satisfaction & contentment in your employment. Yet, generally speaking, it is intelligence (measured in IQ & cognitive ability) & a high degree of conscientiousness that determine success within the workplace (7).
It should not be understated here that the ability to work *with* others will have a profound effect on whether one achieves the seamless progress desired within an organization or, equally, as an independent business.
The same is true in the workplace as in life. To exist is to participate in an iterated trading game in which reciprocity & generosity reign supreme.

Despite some rigorous planning, there is no rigid career path - especially if you aren't absolutely convinced on where you want to go & what you want to do. Always remain open to opportunity, regardless of whether you are trying to progress in one specific industry, or one specific company, or even if you are happy where you currently are. You never know what might present itself if you keep your eyes open.

You have to start somewhere. This chapter has, up until now, covered that. But where you are headed, who knows? Even with your career mapped out there is sure to be some bumps in the road, some hurdles to overcome & some unexpected avenues to go down.

Allow me to present you with the following analogy: Imagine entering a house... you don't know what's on the inside, but you have taken the initiative to open the door & find out. The hallway opens up & you begin to make your way through. There are no doors present but there is a staircase. You climb the staircase for a while, progressing one step at a time.

Upon reaching the top of the staircase there is a door. You open it. The room is dark, you cannot see, but you stumble forward. After a while you come to a wall & can go no further.

Reaching around, you find a doorknob on the adjacent wall. Slowly opening the door, you enter a new room. This one is far different to the ones before. Light & vibrant, you feel yourself uplifted as you pass through. However, as you get further into the room it begins to smell & it appears to be getting smaller & smaller. Before long the smell is too much... it's hard to breathe & you can barely move in such a confined space! Beginning to panic, you rush back to the door, only to realise it is no longer there.

You search for a way out. Frantically feeling for the original door, you notice a small gap on the floor. A trap door! Swiftly opening the door, you hurry down to this new room. Here you find a space that settles your anxiety. It's not too colourful but isn't dull. It's not too spacious but isn't claustrophobic like the one before. It doesn't smell of roses but doesn't have any peculiar odour either. This room feels right, it feels comfortable, it feels safe. This room is where you stay, content & at peace, knowing that this place is the one you will play out the rest of your days in.

Translation:
The house is a metaphor for the job/career ladder & also for the psychological undertones that result through changes in career trajectory (& life in general). Admittedly, I did go slightly overboard with the details. However, I tried to make it seem more realistic to the career path many of us will find ourselves in.

Perhaps you were able to acknowledge this from the staircase symbolising progression within a specific job/career. Your career will take some twists & turns. Your interests may change. The fundamental reality, & the psychological underpinnings of your life, may chaotically traverse to a place (physical or metaphorical) that you are as yet unprepared for.
There are untold variables that will reveal themselves in both your professional & personal life. One part of your life (&/or your career) may seem perfect for a while – hence the vibrant room after the dark one. This makes us feel safe, secure & in order. However, as you read above,

that 'room' changed pretty quickly as you progressed through it!

Sometimes, what is right for us at one point in time turns out to be quite the opposite as we continue to move through life. Finally, after going through many different 'rooms', you find the one that you settle on.
Can I say this for certain? Absolutely not.
Every person has a different life & an untold quantity of variables that simply cannot be prepared for. However, this analogy will hold true for many &, if nothing else, is a good general outline for how your work, & perhaps your life, will unfold.

This central focus of career progression within a specific job/company has led to the formulation of the term, '*The Quarter-Life Crisis*'.
Coined by British comedian Jimmy Carr, in his book 'Before & Laughter', it is explained in the following passage:
"*A quarter life crisis is about finding your purpose. See 'Trainspotting', 'Fight Club' and 'The Matrix' and for heaven's sake, take the red pill. The cliché of the quarter life crisis is travelling: you go on an adventure to 'find yourself' and what you discover is: wherever you go, there you are. When you travel, you become acutely aware you are a story you tell yourself. In my story I was twenty-five, bored, frustrated and wanting a life less ordinary. So, I changed my life and became a stand-up comedian.*

When I was twenty-five I thought I was terribly old to discover that I wanted to be a comedian. Twenty-five seems incredibly young now, but when you're twenty-five, that's the oldest you've ever been – it's a personal best. And if things aren't going according to plan, if you don't even have a plan, twenty-five feels horribly old. It's easy to look back on my life and think, 'That's the only way it could've gone.' But I'm acutely aware it could've gone another way" (8).

This is the experience many men have in their late 20's/early 30's where they have climbed the corporate ladder, only to realise that it was based on the false premise that this was what they wanted for their life. Essentially, they climbed to the top of the ladder, only to realise it was leant against the wrong wall.
Further, as Jimmy Carr once again so eloquently put it, *"people climb to a position & they think happiness is going to live there… & I think you'll be better served trying to make yourself happy & then worry about where you're going"* (9).
In fact, evidence of this mental model can be dated all the way back to the Stoics; *"man has two lives & the second begins when he realizes he only has one"* – Confucius.
Who are we to argue with an age-old insight like that?

Work-Life Balance?
Your identity is not limited to your work of course. Nevertheless, your job/career will take up a large amount of your life, so it is worth taking due consideration of this.

If your job may take up say 50% of your life (& that is particularly generous today) what else makes up *'you'*? Determining your job/career prospects & understanding where your personality sits in the 'Big 5' is just one piece of the puzzle.

Remember an earlier allusion to work/life balance? Well let's take a moment to rethink that idea.

Ask someone what they want in a job & you will frequently receive the answer "a good work/life balance". Often, this will look like a day job that spans the (informally referred to) 9-5. Each of us are now painfully aware that working days are rarely 9-5, yet this serves as a general outline. This 9-5 will still consume ~40hours per week in which to work. Whilst the ability to find a job that you are passionate about & that you find purposeful cannot be understated, I want to bring your attention here to incorporating the many other aspects of life *alongside* your work.

Failure to nurture these other aspects of life could be catastrophic.

There exists a large number of men (this may soon include women with the increase of women in the workplace) who have purchased a ticket to this lottery & who have worked tirelessly to manufacture success in employment, industry & socioeconomic status. These are, of course, positive outcomes in & of themselves. Yet, many of these 'high performers' have a life that is completely out of synchronicity with the rest of the world. Some will have crippling dependencies & deadly coping mechanisms. Others end up having no friendships or intimate relationship/s. A few result in a permanent state of anxiety & fear of losing everything, which prevents them from ever taking a day off from working. They cannot switch off.

We must acknowledge that there are other areas to life of equal importance. They may not seem that way to you now, but rest assured, if you do not give adequate care & respect to these other areas, they will likely lead to suffering at a later stage.
By the end of this book many of these areas will have been addressed. It will require a substantial degree of introspection & self-reflection. At times it may become uncomfortable. Keep a pen & paper handy, they will be good company as you progress through the book.

If, at any point, you become troubled or concerned with what you uncover, or if you feel as though you require professional support, please do not hesitate to seek help & assistance from a trained medical professional & to speak to friends & family who can also assist with your wellbeing.
I must add here that this book does not constitute any formal, legal contract or working relationship, nor does it provide any health or medical advice.
For more information, please refer back to the disclaimer at the beginning of the book.

Ponder these few questions before reading on:

How do you intend to conduct yourself & your life in relation to your family, to your friends & to an intimate partner?

How will you look after your physical, mental & emotional wellbeing?

How will you develop new skills & ideas, improving your current skillset & your potential capabilities across the lifespan?

How will you integrate & serve within your community?

What kind of relationships do you want from your friends & intimate partner/s?

Communicate this to yourself & be concise. If you don't know exactly what you expect or want to see in these relationships, grab another piece of paper & a pen. This time, rather than noting down the things you take particular pleasure in or find yourself responding in disgust to, begin to write down what your fixed boundaries are.

First, do this for your friendships. Then, on a separate page, write down what your fixed boundaries are for your intimate partner/s. These are the things you consider to be categorically non-negotiable for your relationships. Once you have done that, write down what you are totally okay with (or even what traits & behaviours you are ideally looking for). Again, repeat this for each. Finally, write down the things that sit somewhere in the middle for you. These things are not fixed boundaries, but nor are they things you are totally okay with. This area are the things that you *can* tolerate but that are less-than-ideal, respectfully.

People often refrain from doing activities like this for several reasons. Firstly, it is particularly uncomfortable to have these honest, vulnerable discussions with another human being, even if that human being is yourself in the beginning.

Additionally, it shines a light on things that we are partially aware of but try to shrug off or dismiss. For example, a girlfriend or boyfriend who is openly flirting, or perhaps even cheating, with another person. Or a friend who encourages you to waste time drinking every weekend when you want to be working on a project or doing something more productive.

Potentially worse still, thought activities like this can unsettle the very foundations from which your identity lays. If we shine a light on our environment & do so in a manner that every corner of the room becomes visible, we may just find some nasty creatures lurking in the spaces we are least willing to look.

The impact of technological change

In the Western world we have applied virtue to being busy. We are today becoming painfully aware that it is our immediate surroundings (family, friends, relationships) that become neglected as a result. Emerging data is shining a light on how it is the quality of our close relationships that play a profound role in our overall wellbeing (10)(11). However, our social lives have been subject to immense change through the last few decades, with the digital/technological revolution/4th Industrial revolution at the epicentre of modern society. It is largely through this change & subsequent decline in physical, interpersonal relationships that we are beginning to uncover just how important our social relationships are to our overall health &, dare I say, happiness. So important, in fact, is social connection that I have devoted an entire chapter to the topic later in this book.

The digital revolution of the last decade or two has seen the world become rapidly interconnected through technological advancements &, as a result, has caused some people to proclaim statements such as "life online & death in reality". It is clear that we are undergoing radical change in our world &, perhaps as a result of our digital interconnectedness, we have become even more fragmented & lonely in our day-to-day lives. Whilst correlation does not necessarily mean causation, this tumultuous trend of loneliness in the 21st century poses its own problems for us as individuals.

Loneliness *"is reported to be more dangerous than smoking; high degree of loneliness precipitates suicidal ideation & para-suicide, Alzheimer's disease, & other dementia, & adversely affects the immune & cardio-vascular system. It is a generally accepted opinion that loneliness results in a decline of well-being & has an adverse effect on physical health, possibly through immunologic impairment or neuro-endocrine changes"* (12).

Despite this, it is important to realise that our recent innovations (smart phones, apps & social media) are all tools &, like any tool, can be used for your benefit or for your detriment. With these websites & digital applications, it is important to realize that *you* are the product. These companies want your attention & will do everything in their power to achieve it.

Now would be a good time to take a moment to recognize *how* you are perceiving these technologies (& the world). Are you using them or are they using you?

These new technologies are not only likely here to stay but will continue to evolve & play a larger role in our day-to-day lives. Can you utilize our new technological innovations, whilst managing to nurture the relationships in your life, & simultaneously retain the ability to remain productive to your community? Perhaps you are even able to improve these aspects?

Can you find a way to use it to enhance the relationships in your life & your own productivity in service to others? This integration is going to take a considerable amount of effort & discipline on your part, just as it will on mine. Nevertheless, I do see potential here, provided we are disciplined in our use of these immensely powerful tools.

How we respond to the world can either be immensely empowering or absolutely debilitating. *You* have the power to make your life a perfect paradise or a living hell. With great power comes great responsibility. Abdication of the latter can wreak havoc on your life. You have to become aware (perhaps painfully so) that it is *you* who is responsible for your suffering &, likewise, for your happiness too.

How are you perceiving yourself? How are you perceiving the world?

"Nothing is good or bad, but thinking makes it so" - Hamlet, William Shakespeare.

Equally, our internal dialogue shapes our world. Simple adjustments in how we speak to ourselves can dramatically shift our perspective. Bruce Lee once said, *"never speak negatively of yourself, even as a joke, your body doesn't know the difference"*.

Nuanced differences in your language, such as changing from "I *am* sad" to "I *feel* sad" directs the statement away from your identity & instead presents the concept as something you are experiencing. It is not 'who' you are. We could even take this one step further & state "I feel sad *right now*". This shows us that it is a temporary feeling, something that is occurring in the present &, as such, is not permanent.

There is a fantastic analogy you can use here; if you think of your mind as the sky & think of your emotions/feelings as the weather. The sky is omnipresent, it is always there regardless of the weather. The weather, however, changes from day to day, possibly even moment to moment. The weather never stays the same &, as such, we should never expect our emotions to stay fixed & rigid. We (as the sky) observe the weather but need not feel obliged to indulge in the ongoing changes in our emotional state.

To put this in the relevant context; "this current feeling is something I am experiencing at this precise moment in time... *This too shall pass*".

Acknowledgment of a feeling is often the first step to personal development & growth, but more on that later.

Purpose & Responsibility

"There's a moment when every boy realizes no one is coming to save him. And that's when he becomes a man. And some boys never get there and stay children forever" (13).

What do you want from your life?
What is going to make your life worthwhile?
What is it that will get you through the difficult times when they inevitably arrive in your life?
What will allow you to endure life, with all its suffering?
Take a moment to truly ponder those questions before continuing.

Humans are fundamentally drawn to 'do' something &, whilst we can explore the idea of taking time away from '*doing*' & into time spent '*being*' later (after all, we are human beings), it is the pursuit of a higher value/goal that brings about positive emotion. When times are difficult, it isn't happiness that will keep you going. You must have something deeper pushing you forward.
Don't aim for happiness, aim for purpose & meaning.
As the great philosopher Friedrich Nietzsche proclaimed; *"He whose life has a why can bear almost any how"* (14).

In Dr Jordan Peterson's pivotal book '12 rules for life', rule 7 is appropriately titled *"pursue what is meaningful (not what is expedient)"* (15).
Later in the same chapter (or rule, as Peterson puts it) we read, *"Pain and suffering define the world. Of that, there*

can be no doubt. Sacrifice can hold pain and suffering in abeyance, to a greater or lesser degree – and greater sacrifices can do that more effectively than lesser. Of that, there can be no doubt. Everyone holds this knowledge in their soul. Thus, the person who wants to alleviate suffering – who wishes to rectify the flaws in Being; who wants to bring about the best of all possible futures; who wants to create Heaven on Earth - will make the greatest of sacrifices, of self and child, of everything that is loved, to live a life aimed at the Good. He will forgo expediency. He will pursue the path of ultimate meaning. And he will in that manner bring salvation to the ever-desperate world" (16).

You could consider what it would be like to be void of a 'why'. You may even be in this position currently. If there is no reason to do anything then why do anything at all? If life is pointless, or perhaps oppressive & tyrannical, then why should you play along?
This rhetoric is becoming increasingly internalised in men today. The result... catastrophic.

A staggering number of boys are falling behind in education & are bailing out of the universities at an alarming rate. A poignant piece in The Guardian, back in 2016, raises the alarm here.
The article begins, *"Men are less likely to go to British universities, those who do are more likely to drop out and those who complete their course are less likely to get a good degree...*

The report, entitled Boys to Men: The Underachievement of Young Men In Higher Education and How to Start Tackling It, says the proportion of men entering UK higher education institutions is at a record low. In 2015, the gap between the sexes was a record 9.2 percentage points, meaning women are now 35% more likely to go to university than men" (17).

Further, *"Girls are outperforming boys at every level, from elementary school through graduate school... Between 1999 & 2019, the percentage of 16-24 year old males participating in the workforce fell 17% & that number is projected to decrease even more over the next 10 years"* (18).

These men all have the potential to be respectable members of society, perhaps even the structural pillars of their community someday. Failure to take on this responsibility, however, will leave a void – in both society & within themselves. If these individuals are presented with a world where there is no hope, no meaning & no reason to become something more than they currently are, they will find themselves descending to the depths of hell.

A life of Peter Pan awaits men who have no reason to grow up & take their place in the world.

Psycho-therapeutic fields & the absence of male role models

In reference to the current state of men's mental health, author, comedian & political commentator Konstantin Kisin makes the following groundbreaking statement;

"most of the personal development & psychology fields are geared towards female ways of being, & most of the ways we treat, for example, depression. Men don't need the same thing as women do when it comes to that. What men need is to feel powerful & capable. The reason you are not the greatest threat to you is that you feel in charge of your life. That's what men need to pursue with every fibre of their being. You need to struggle, you need to fight, & you need to achieve".

Kisin continued by contending that, *"I'm someone who has been depressed at points in my life & it's not because 'I was having a mental health problem', it's because my life was shit, & I was shit. So what men need is to pursue their dreams, to fight & struggle, & to achieve"* (19).

The above extract is not a one-size-fits-all approach & Kisin is not a psychologist, psychiatrist or mental health first aider. Nevertheless, there is some efficacy in what he is saying as it would appear that men & women generally respond differently to therapeutic protocols & counselling. For example, a systematic review showed that *"interventions that appear to improve male help-seeking incorporate role-models, psychoeducational materials, symptom recognition and management skills, active problem-solving tasks, motivating behaviour change, signposting materials, and content that builds on positive masculine traits (e.g., responsibility and strength)"* (20).

In our culture today, as well as the female-dominated social & therapeutic fields, the message is very much for a man or woman to accept where they are right now & to be happy with it... that there *should* be no reason for you to feel the way you currently do, *if only you could see your inherent value*.

To be clear, I am not saying there isn't some efficacy in this statement. You do have an inherent level of worth & you do need to accept where you currently are in your life. But this is not the message (at least not in totality) that men need to hear.

Men want, dare I say *need*, a path forward... someone to say "No, you're not all that you could be, *& you know it*".

What benefits women does not necessarily benefit men, & vice versa.

I have my suspicion that our current state of counselling, therapy & self-help is making men feel okay with their objective level of mediocrity & their current set of circumstances, as opposed to lighting a fire within them to pursue a better life for themselves. Though there are undoubtedly benefits to therapy for men, I do wonder whether we would be better encouraging men to step into the ever-growing void of their inherent masculinity... a masculinity that is so often repressed today.

This requires action. It necessitates forward motion. It aims up.

Men look towards suitable role models from which to aspire. The responsibility rests upon each of us to embody the archetype of a strong role model.

Perhaps you have kids yourself. Maybe you don't. Regardless as to whether you chose the position or not, it is very likely that there is somebody out there looking toward you to set an example. Whether you are aware of this or not, you must set an example & set it well.

Could this be a better course of action to generate an army of men? Men who create a better life for their partners, their families & their communities?

Of course, there will be some negative pushback on these points, of which I'm open to. Not least the idea of an 'army' of men sounding particularly threatening. I stand by this choice of wording. What does an army do? It fights for you, it defends you, it protects you. What do our families, our communities & our world need? People who will fight for it, defend it, protect it. With the correct messaging & shift in public consciousness, would this not be beneficial?

I could be completely wrong in the assumption that men require a differing approach here than women do, though I suspect we will come to understand this area far better in the future.

Whilst this book will address many different aspects of masculinity & a route forward in life, it is not a specific plan or personal advice. If you are struggling with your mental health, it is always important that you seek professional support, alongside that of your friends & family, provided this is possible. For more information, please refer back to the disclaimer at the start of the book.

Victim mentality

Let's talk about something that plagues our collective consciousness, & our culture at large, today. Yes, I'm referring to the ever-present victim mentality.

Some people *may* have a better start position. Some people are born into wealth or have a family business or land in which they will inherit. Some people will have a stable, nuclear family & adequate support network during their childhood. Others are less fortunate. Life isn't perfect. You don't get to choose your starting point. Like anything, it is not about where you start in life that determines where you end up. But one thing is for sure; by abdicating responsibility over your own life, you will pay the price... one way or another.

Further, holding up the victim card as some signifier of moral virtue is not a sufficient long-term strategy to yield success or personal fulfilment.

Let it be made strikingly clear, ascribing yourself the identity of being oppressed does not make you virtuous, it just makes you a victim. Perceiving yourself as being oppressed & a victim will allow your ideology to persist but, whilst you place blame on the world, there are other individuals who are taking responsibility for their own lives & are consciously working to make themselves better.

Who do you think has a better chance of success?

"instead of claiming your status is victim, which is self-evident... yes, victim, obviously... life is fundamentally suffering, & it's contaminated by malevolence, & that's a permanent reality.

Instead of characterizing yourself as a hapless victim, differentially affected by that & then looking for whose fault it is, you do something radical & you think "maybe it's not my fault, maybe it's my responsibility to do something about that".

There's plenty of suffering in the world that you could do something about. You could start with your own for that matter, you could treat yourself half decently. That's rule 2 right, 'treat yourself like you're someone responsible for helping'. You could try that. It actually works quite nicely. And if you can manage that, well maybe you can do the same for your family. That would be a nice extension of grace, let's say. And maybe if you get good at that, well you can try doing it for the whole community.

You could take on the load of that suffering, the load of that victimization, let's say. You could take that on, not only as an unavoidable existential reality, but as a challenge to the deepest part of yourself" (21).

There will, no doubt, be people who still look at the world & decide not to take action, not to aim at the highest possible values, they will not dare to be great. No one escapes life without going through harmful experiences, without facing some kind of emotional pain, without experiencing some degree of suffering.

Dr Peterson took it one step further when he proclaimed that *"life is suffering"* (22).

Who wants that?

Under such circumstances wouldn't anyone turn to simple hedonistic pleasure? Wouldn't anybody seek an escape to Neverneverland? There has to be something to compensate for the misery of existence... doesn't there?

This suffering I speak of could come in one of many forms. However, if you were never faced with any suffering, if you never had to overcome any hardship in life, there would be nothing to you. We will all have battles in life, some will come from the outside world & some will come from within our own psyche. It is through difficulty & struggle that the 'potential you' can come to fruition.

One day you will look back at some of the darkest days, some of the toughest moments in your life, & be grateful that they happened. Without them much of you would still be lying dormant, unconscious, unawakened.

It can feel comforting to believe that God has a plan. I am not going to say that there isn't some utility in that. Further, this is neither a book advocating for, nor is it one fighting against religion. If faith plays a positive role in your life, have at it!

We will touch upon faith later in the book as it relates to the noble aim & the pursuit of a highest value.

Nevertheless, if you are going to change or improve your life, it is you who must make the conscious decision to take full responsibility & full accountability for your life.

"It's the noble aim... & what is that? Well, it was encapsulated in part in the story of Marda. It's to pay attention, it's to speak properly, it's to confront chaos, it's to make a better world, something like that. And that's

enough of a noble aim so that you can stand up without cringing at the very thought of your own existence, so that you can do something that's worthwhile & justify your wretched position on the planet" (23).

If you want to improve yourself as a person you must address your past, assess the present, & profess your future. That is a fancy way of saying; show yourself what you have done, who you currently are & what you could become, should you take the appropriate steps.
Set out a plan. Where will you be in five years?
What could your life look like if you took responsibility for your actions & orchestrated your life towards the highest possible values?

"One forty-something client told me his vision, formulated by his younger self: "I see myself retired, sitting on a tropical beach, drinking margaritas in the sunshine."
That's not a plan. That's a travel poster. After eight margaritas, you're only fit to await the hangover. After three weeks of margarita-filled days, if you have any sense, you're bored stiff & self-disgusted. In a year, or less, you're pathetic."" (24).

The bottom line;
Don't aim for happiness, aim for purpose & meaning.

Masculinity

What is a masculine man?
What traits does he embody?
How is he perceived by others?
More importantly, how does he perceive himself?
"You should be a monster, an absolute monster, & then you should learn how to control it". That emphatic statement was professed by Dr Jordan Peterson on 'The Joe Rogan Experience' back in 2016 (25).

The now infamous line may appear to be destructive & malevolent on the surface but, when embodied correctly, may just be the most liberating statement ever to be articulated regarding masculinity.
We are so quick as a culture to discourage aggression & assertiveness & to encourage, conversely, passivity & conformity... almost to the point of blind co-operation. Co-operation in-and-of-itself is a great attribute to hold when it comes to relationships & existing in the social world. Perhaps too is conformity in some respects. However, this falls apart when subjected to tyranny & oppression. You have to be able to say "no" when it needs to be said.

It is no small feat to become aware of your capacity for harm – for what you are capable of under certain circumstances. Yet, it is essential for you to understand this in order to be a good man.

Building upon Dr Peterson's spectacular statement (above) we bear witness to a strikingly similar message in a later podcast conversation, again involving Jordan Peterson, this time with US Navy veteran, Jocko Willink. Here Dr Peterson states: *"A harmless man is not a good man, a good man is a very, very dangerous man who has that under voluntary control"* (26).

What can we take from this?
A man's life is suffering, it is pain, it is struggle. That doesn't mean give up. That means rise to the challenge, take on responsibility, live a life of meaning & purpose.
"Life can be happiness... if you're a woman or a dog" (27).
Love, happiness, sunshine & rainbows; that isn't what constitutes a productive, fulfilling life. That is what you witness in a fairytale, or a book or a film. As a man you have to bring something to the table. You have to put yourself out there & earn your success.
Women can just be... Men have to become.

Your pursuits will determine the quality of your life. As the old saying goes, "It's better to be a warrior in a garden than a gardener in a war".
It is better to prepare for every eventuality than to under-prepare & get obliterated by the inevitable challenges & suffering caused by life. Failure to prepare yourself adequately can be catastrophic. Why?
Because whether you like it or not, to be alive means that, by definition, you are all in. Further, consider a rather simple yet unbelievably potent quote – one to

cement into the very fabric of your brain – from Jerzy Gregorek:

"Hard choices, easy life. Easy choices, hard life".

Traditionally, cultures across the globe have participated in 'rites of passage' practices. How do we celebrate a boy becoming a man today? We give him a certificate of academic achievement (or more common today, *lack* of academic achievement) (17)(18) & tell him to get a job. What I am insinuating here is that our culture woefully underprepares boys to step into manhood, whether that is from an institutional standpoint (the school system) or through the family & wider societal influence.
We fail to give young men any responsibility, nor a sense of belonging, within their community.
There are many good 'games' to play in society (plumber, electrician, father etc), yet we fail to present these as potential opportunities for long-term life satisfaction. They simply aren't made to be attractive. Instead, we practically force young men into the opposite... simple, hedonistic pleasure.

Gamification
An interesting mental model that could go some way to rectifying this issue is the idea of 'gamifying' life.
If we look at the overwhelming desire of men to partake in video games, we can begin to draw on the underpinning psychology to order our lives in a more productive manner. As George Mack recounts on the subject, *"in the modern age there's such a lack of meaning, & the one thing that video games do insanely*

well is there's so much meaning when people are playing them". Mack continues with the following assessment, *"why is there such a dichotomy of people that are such good video game players but then have such terrible time at life... well is it a well-designed video game?"* (28).

The 'gamification' of life would seem to hold some merit. If an individual can be more thoroughly engaged in their life, they will likely reap the benefits down the line. To be successful you first must *want* to play.

Life may not appear as enthralling as a video game on the surface, & I am certainly not advising you to stir up controversy or act unlawfully in order to generate that heightened, dramatized effect gaming has. However, strategizing life into levels & objectives to be met, or overcome, will very likely result in an elevated level of engagement.

In practice, just as you wouldn't climb a ladder by jumping onto the fourth or fifth rung, you must calculate each iteration of the 'game' that will allow you to climb up one step at a time.

Aim too high & risk feeling like a failure for not succeeding. Aim too low & fail to test your capabilities & develop your skillset. Aim to be just a little bit better, however, & you can play forever.

Whilst strategizing your life into a structure that resembles that of a video game, it would be wrong for me not to mention the effects of video games (& other

activities that constitute a stimulating environment) on your current, & ambient, levels of dopamine.
"Dopamine is a neurotransmitter that plays a role in pleasure, motivation, & learning" (29). You will frequently read about dopamine in this book as it plays a substantial role in not just obtaining goals, but the very pursuit of them. As Dr Robert Sapolsky has recently proclaimed, *"it's not the pursuit of happiness, but it's the happiness of the pursuit"* (30).

Leveraging dopamine is a super-skill. Here, however, I want to allude to the stimulating environment of the modern man (& woman for that matter). Many of us fail to appreciate just how stimulating & arousing our current environment actually is. Just a generation or two ago, most individuals did not have access to information at their fingertips like we do today; mobile phones & other digital devices were virtually non-existent, social media was years away, yet to manifest into anything tangible.

The virtual world that we know today, modern video gaming & instant messaging, was unfathomable. The television & radio were popular, but they had few channels & were not assimilated into our everyday lives the way the digital world is today.
The point I am making here is that none of the above were as 'limbically hijacking' as they are today. Images & acts of a sexual or provocative manner were not common & the media companies did not have the psychological data that they have today in order to capture & captivate

the audience, keeping them hooked on the hedonic treadmill, so to speak.

All of the above leave us in a constant state of stimulation. We are constantly aroused & in an elevated state, not dissimilar to the anticipation of a goal or achievement.

Take some time to allow your dopamine levels to reset to a more harmonious level (i.e. back to baseline). If you are always stimulated, you are always loading on the dopaminergic system. Dopamine, however, cannot *stay* elevated &, following an elevation above baseline, you can expect to take a fall back below baseline, in order to eventually re-adjust back to your baseline level.

In her book 'Dopamine Nation' & in her online lecture for 'The Weekend University' (referenced below) Dr Anna Lembke advises taking a 30-day dopamine fast in order to obtain a complete dopamine reset (31).

Dopamine is neither good or bad. Like anything, it ultimately comes down to how you are cultivating your environment & how you are choosing to act & behave in the world. Understanding how to leverage dopamine will however be immensely beneficial when it comes to moving towards your goals & objectives.

Cultivating a path forward

We have grown accustomed to men 'failing to launch' in this generation, whether that be in a career, in their relationship/s or across their life in general. Without a path forward from childhood & adolescence we are pretty much guaranteeing this outcome.

This evident failure to acculturate young men leaves them with little choice in where they find their sense of belonging. Men tend to gravitate toward certain groups to develop & shape their identity &, just as there are good groups to join (mentors, teammates, friendships, family etc), there are also some not so good groups in our world.

Positive pathways tend to lead to personal growth & the potential for long term success in life. Groups that are aiming down however, committing crime & engaging in destructive behaviours (alcohol, drugs, crime etc), have little, if any, future prospects.

This is unfortunately compounded by our culture. We demonise the symptoms without addressing the underlying cause/s. I am not saying here that any of the resulting behaviours are inevitable or even acceptable. In fact, it is every individuals' responsibility for enacting change in their own lives & to choose their own attitudes & behaviours.

We must hold ourselves to a higher standard. Yes, the circumstances may be difficult. Yes, the path forward may be grey & unclear. This does not mean that we should abdicate responsibility. Each & every one of us must take accountability for how we conduct ourselves in the world, providing a positive example for others to follow.

In an environment that is decaying & lacking positive role models, the pathway that many men go down tend to be both catastrophic for themselves & for society as a whole. These avenues (& the groups that find themselves immersed in them) lack inspiration, motivation & meaning. As a result, they end up wasting their existence away, one hopeless day at a time.

If you perceive yourself as being one of these individuals & you're reading this, it might be time to take a step back & look at your surroundings.

Who are your role models? Who are you spending time with? Are your actions in alignment with your values?

James Clear has a great passage in his book 'Atomic Habits' where he addresses this subject area. Clear states, *"Surround yourself with people who have the habits you want to have yourself"* (32). *"Join a culture where your desired behaviour is the normal behaviour"* (33).

What are you doing that is productive... productive both for you & for society? Where are you currently situated in life & where you could you be if you had a goal, formulated a plan, & took aim at the highest possible values?

"You don't have to be the victim of your environment. You can also be the architect of it" (34).

Finally, & most emphatically, you must understand the following sentiment: *"True hell is when the person you are, meets the person you could have been"* (35).

Whilst touching on the topic of role models, it is important to avoid falling into the trap of assuming that, just because somebody has achieved wild levels of success in one particular area of life, they are truly fulfilled or are living a life of peace, harmony & contentment. Many of us look outwards toward a role model; an idealized vision of 'potential you', perhaps even the epitome of perfection. We begin to think that if we could be them, or at least get to the position they are in, we will have 'made it'… we will be happy.

There are a few problems with this assumption.
Firstly, happiness is not dependent on external factors. Even the pursuit of happiness is a flawed concept… you are literally telling yourself that you are *not* happy! This is what's referred to as the 'backwards law'.
The pursuit of losing weight solidifies the fact that you aren't at a weight or body composition that you would like. The goal of improving your social skills re-enforces the fact that your social life/social skills are not at the level you believe to be adequate.
The backwards law is an interesting frame to run through when deciding on what goals you are looking to pursue & whether they actually are 'your' goals, as opposed to goals that have been culturally/societally influenced. It also considers both the aim that you are motivated towards, as well as the current circumstance that you are seeking to drive away from.

Further, when it comes to your role models, you don't get to change just one variable. You cannot cherry-pick the success they have in their specific field (wealth, attraction, skill, fame etc) without taking the rest of the metaphorical pie. You don't just get the success & the stardom, you also get the crippling anxiety, the failed marriage & the kids who hate you. You don't just get the fame & adulation, you also get the fear of insufficiency, the crippling loneliness, the physical & psychological pain, the sleepless nights & the addictions to drugs/alcohol/gambling/women etc.

Ask yourself; Do you really want to have what they have? Do you really want to swap your life with theirs?
The chances are, you wouldn't &, moreover, you shouldn't.
Once you finish this book it is my hope that you are able to organise your life in a way that makes *you* the success... that makes you the hero in your own life. Or, as emphatically stated by podcaster, comedian & commentator, Joe Rogan, *"live your life like you're the hero in your movie"* (36).

Change is hard. It involves unlearning old behaviours & integrating new ones. This may seem overwhelming to begin with, especially if the magnitude of difference between where you currently are & where you want to be is far greater than you would like. You see who you could be & you see who you currently are... there is a gigantic discrepancy there. That is okay.
Don't base your day one off of someone else's day one hundred. You can minimize the psychological burden of this by moving your vision away from the idealized end result & closer to the present moment.
"Compare yourself to who you were yesterday, not who someone else is today" (37).

Where are you right now? What is one thing, no matter how small, that you could do today to move yourself 1% closer to your desired outcome?

You'd be amazed at what a 1% improvement can make across a long enough timescale. Start small & be consistent.

I have a motto that I live by; *"1% better every single day"*.

"Who could you be if you stopped doing the thing/s that are wasting your time, draining your energy & that are taking you further away from your goal/s? Who could you be if you looked at the suffering & terror of life, without becoming bitter & resentful, & voluntarily carried your part of the load?" (38).

Life is suffering

Many good people will tussle & fight their way up the ladder or hierarchy, or whatever you want to term it, with untold obstacles in their way. When somebody says, "life is suffering" this is partly what they mean (not to mention the chaos & destruction when things go wrong, when someone trespasses us, when we are deceived, when we suffer heartbreak & so on).

It is the act of moving forward against the odds, keeping faith in themselves or in something higher as they struggle onwards.

If you take an honest assessment of how you're behaving, what your values are, & whether you are truly serving 'God' (the highest value), perhaps you would not become

bitter & resentful... perhaps you would be rewarded rather than punished...
Perhaps life is a mirror, reflecting the truth of your soul.

The feeling of imposter syndrome is inevitable with any change, whether in your career, your geographical location, your hobbies & so on. This is largely due to the fact that, when you start something new you literally are an imposter... you don't know anything yet. The magnitude of difference between who you currently are & who you aim to become can be startling, to say the least. Again, that is okay. The ground is shaking beneath your feet, but with belief in your chosen path & belief in yourself, you can take another step forward.
"It is not the 10,000th hour that makes you elite, it's the 9,999 that came before it" – Jack Keyworth (myself, as far as I'm aware).

It can be a vulnerable place when you are starting out at something. Your ego will feel threatened & will present you with resistance, all in an attempt to keep you safe. Nevertheless, a 'safe' life is not necessarily a 'good' life. Safety can provide a steady path through life, but it can greatly limit the potential for opportunity & personal growth. As Bruce Lee said, *"do not pray for an easy life, pray for the strength to endure a difficult one"*.
How you feel should not change what you do. Yes, how you feel matters, & yes, you should pay attention to what you are feeling. However, you are not always going to be motivated to do what is required.

Motivation is great when it's there. As David Goggins said in a phenomenal podcast with Chris Williamson, *"that's some kindling to the fire"* (39).

The former Navy Seal, ultra endurance athlete & author continued, *"Motivation's just a word, you have to have these different things in your mind on where you want to go & know that motivation's not going to get me there... I'm not going to always be motivated"* (39).

As a man you must execute regardless of how you're feeling.

Another former Seal, US veteran Jocko Willink, put it emphatically when he said, *"motivation is a feeling that comes & goes, & it doesn't matter if it's there or not. Discipline is infinitely more important. No matter how you feel, get up & do what you are supposed to do."* (40).

It is voluntary exposure to an experience, or an environment, that increases an individual's bravery & develops their confidence. If somebody suffers from agoraphobia, social anxiety disorder or something similar, it is through a process of gradual, voluntary exposure to the 'thing' which develops the strength needed to overcome such an obstacle.

A great explanation of this process is found in Jordan Peterson's conversation with Joe Rogan on the JRE podcast. He states that, *"the clinical literature indicates quite clearly that you don't make people less anxious by doing that, you make them braver"* (25).

Whilst I detest the cliché of "life begins at the edge of your comfort zone", I do feel it pertinent to say that, in a world full of 'safe spaces', make sure you are still tiptoeing out of the comfortable sphere of order & into the difficulty presented in the chaos of life every so often. This will undoubtedly help you develop your character as you progress through life.

A harrowing depiction of life's struggle (& in this specific case, a mothers' struggle) can be seen in Michelangelo's 'La Pieta'.
Presenting a statue of Mary with (a now adult) Christ in her arms, he is on her lap, broken & destroyed.
"You might lose your body out there in the world, but if you stay here you lose your soul" says Jordan Peterson when talking about the role of the mother in allowing her son to go out into the danger & uncertainty of the world (41).
It might feel comfortable living in the comfort of safety & security, but it is an insufficient strategy for a thriving, fulfilled life.

Anxiety will hijack the brain & take you to the worst possible outcome, it will over-estimate the magnitude of the problem & under-estimate your ability to deal with it. This all serves a purpose. It is an evolved response, designed to protect us from danger & imminent threat. However, our lives today bear little resemblance to the environments we evolved from &, as such, we can often find ourselves slipping into a fight or flight, survival response based off circumstances that lack any real fundamental threat to our survival. When anxiety strikes, remind yourself of the following: *"if it's not life threatening, it is just truly ego threatening"* (42).

I'm going to present an analogy here...
We often perceive ourselves as a tree; broad & stable, surrounded by other trees, in our natural environment. We are deeply rooted in the ground, which helps us combat all adverse weather conditions. Yet, when the seasons change or when the unpredictable happens, we lose one leaf... & another... & another. We suddenly feel uneasy. We desperately try to save our leaves from falling, from being blown around chaotically in the wind. We become tight & rigid, resisting life from taking its natural course. Our effort is futile. Our leaves, whilst part of us, are now gone. Will they return? Perhaps, some day. It is acceptance of this uncertainty that allows us to regain a sense of calm. Eventually our leaves will grow back, but this cycle will carry on indefinitely.
"Tension is who you think you should be. Relaxation is who you are" – Buddhist saying.

"We eternally inhabit order, surrounded by chaos. We eternally occupy known territory, surrounded by the unknown. We experience meaningful engagement when we mediate appropriately between them.
We are adapted, in the deepest Darwinian sense, not to the world of objects, but to the meta-realities of order & chaos, yang & yin. Chaos & order make up the eternal, transcendent environment of the living.

*To straddle that fundamental duality is to be balanced: to
have one foot firmly planted in order & security, & the
other in chaos, possibility, growth & adventure."* (43).

Where are your boundaries?
We briefly covered this earlier. Boundaries will show,
both to yourself & to others, that you have self-respect.
Without boundaries you *will* be walked over. If you fail to
stand for something, you'll fall for anything.
You need to know what you are willing to tolerate & what
is categorically non-negotiable so that you don't find
yourself being trespassed or taken advantage of by
others. What are the things you are willing to tolerate &
things that you are completely okay with?

You should hopefully by now have a list of things that are
fixed boundaries or non-negotiables, for your
relationships. Now we will expand this across every
aspect of our life. These may change over time & will
likely be added to & amended as you progress through
life. For now, what are your non-negotiables for your
relationship/s, for your work, for your friendships, for
your family, for your physical & mental health?
Add to your lists whenever you find something new crop
up. In doing so you will develop a greater understanding
of who you are, what you value &, hopefully as a result,
gain value & respect for yourself.

If you know that something is a non-negotiable for you &
you are being presented with that action or behaviour,
whether that be a tyrannical boss at work, or infidelity

from a partner or spouse, you will now be consciously aware of the occurrence, without the ability to lie to yourself or to omit it altogether. In doing so, you are able to make the decision to confront the behaviour, &/or the person.

At the very least, you will be able to remove yourself from such an environment, justified in doing so, knowing that it does not align with your values & what you are willing to tolerate.

Just as you will find yourself adding to these lists as you progress through life, you may find some things changing & evolving for you as you enter different environments & different stages of life.

Nevertheless, your values are the very foundation of your being & if you go against your own values, you go against you.

If don't value yourself, why would anybody else?

'Inner child' & 'Parts'

"Heal the boy & the man will appear" (44).
Let me say that again; *"Heal the boy & the man will appear"* (44).

"Every man right now has a little boy inside of them that's afraid. There's a little boy that's really hurting. So what this little boy did, because he felt powerless when he was young, is did everything in his power to get it back... to get muscles, to get women, to get success, to get fame, to get money. All these things are trying to nourish this little boy whose afraid & hurting. Once that boy is healed, a warrior is born. A divine masculine is born" (45).

The above quotes are profoundly important to the understanding, acceptance & embodiment of who you are. This is not the identity you play in the social sphere, not the labels that society has thrust upon you... this is who you are at the most fundamental level.
Although the above statement may not resonate for everyone, it provides a great oversight of what I intend to uncover in this chapter.

This chapter is going to address terms such as 'inner child', 'parts', 'trauma' & other emotionally charged areas. This is not to be taken as medical or health advice. As established in the disclaimer at the beginning of the book, this is for entertainment purposes & does not constitute, in any way, a legal, working contract or relationship.

For any issues or queries arising from this section (& any other section of the book) please contact your GP or a medical/healthcare professional who can assist you on a professional, one-to-one basis.

Within each of us exists our inner child. I will switch between describing the 'inner child' & 'parts' throughout this chapter – as it is often referred to in certain forms of therapy.

Some of our 'parts' can get exiled due to a variety of factors in our lives. These can include (though they are certainly not limited to) stress, suffering & trauma. Much of this may have occurred in our childhood. These are appropriately termed 'exiled parts' as we have banished them from our conscious awareness. We want nothing to do with them due to the fact that they can make us feel uncomfortable, unstable, or because they are simply too damn painful.

One of the most disastrous compensations for a hurt inner child is not the chaos or rebellion that flows from a perpetual state of anger & destruction. It is, in fact, quite the contrary. It is the formation of the 'high achiever'.

High achievers

High achievers tend to be motivated by a never-ending desire to succeed. Achievement sounds great on the surface, yet the fuel driving the passion (in this case) is self-destructive. Once their goal is hit, the goalposts move… they can never be satiated. No matter how much they achieve & how good their lives become, they are never finished.

Why?

Because they are not running *towards* their goal. Rather, they are running *away* from something else... something deep-rooted in their subconscious; a failure, an inadequacy, a painful experience, a perceived defect in *who* they are.

You absolutely *can* use this dynamic to drive your performance & to strive for success. Who am I to say that an individual shouldn't use this as fuel for their performance &/or success in a certain endeavour? Many do. Some even become exceptionally successful. In fact, I would go as far to say that, if you find someone who is at the top of their game, leading in their chosen field, or super-rich (in either simple monetary terms or through assets & other income), there's a pretty good chance are they got there by running away from something else. This doesn't mean to say that it is necessarily incorrect or ill-advised. If it works for you, have at it. What I am proposing however, is to develop an awareness of your underlying motivation. Be mindful of what is fuelling your endeavours & make sure they don't end up leaving you burnt out, bitter, & full of hate & regret.

Individuals that are running away from their problems & insecurities are oftentimes using their achievements as a demonstration of being good enough or being worthy of 'love' & 'acceptance'. It can be an attempt to show the world (the world often being the person, or people, who didn't show them when they were young, vulnerable & dependant) that they can be loved... that they are good enough for love.

These external achievements never manage to fill the void that exists inside of them. Not limited to high achievers, workaholics & perfectionists run the same program in their head.

"If I can be perfect, I will be worthy of love & appreciation, *& then I will be okay*".

Perfectionism

Whilst there is no categorical definition of 'perfectionism', there exists a confluence of characteristics which tend to underlie its presence.

Perfectionism is self-destructive. It is essentially the belief that if you were to look perfect & to do everything perfectly, you will somehow avoid or minimize painful feelings, shame & judgement.

Perfectionism is self-destructive because there is no such thing as 'perfect'. Perfectionism is a fundamentally unattainable goal.

The overarching themes of perfectionism include:
1. High achievement/performance standards
2. An "obsessive" approach to improvement
3. Rigid and dichotomous thinking
4. Recurring dissatisfaction with current performances or works (46).

"Perfectionism is procrastination masquerading as quality control" (47).

You are alive. Take a moment to truly feel that. Become aware of the transient nature of existence.

Your life, in evolutionary terms, is over in the blink of an eye. You have a series of sensory experiences & then you are gone.

Do not waste time trying to be perfect (*whatever that is*).

A human balloon... narcissistic co-dependency

Stick with me here!

Balloons must be inflated to stay in the air. An individual who is not complete in & of themselves will struggle to remain airborne. They need other people to continuously re-inflate them. This often presents as a 'needy' person. Sometimes, however, this 'neediness' can become deeply malevolent & narcissistic, with an individual using other people to make themselves feel better – even if it harms the other person. Either way, this failure to have someone else around results in them deflating & crashing to the ground.

Such a person is usually wounded... the air is leaving them at their base. Why else would they be unable to stay afloat like the other balloons?

As a result, they depend on others. However, this portrayal of neediness can only work for so long.

In order to heal their wound & to become like the other balloons, they must learn to tie the knot at their own base. Doing so allows them to hold onto the air, the life-energy, the self-worth if you will, & allows them to float without the dependency on others & without an underlying level of neediness.

A narcissist may inflict untold suffering on others as they use & discard people for their own temporary gain, but ultimately it is they who suffer the most. It is they who have to live like a deflated balloon whilst everyone else around them floats carefree in the world.

Whether it's visible or not, that feeling is there. This is why the narcissist is not met with hate in this book, but with empathy.

There is an important distinction to be had here. Your 'value', or the value ascribed to you by society, does not change your 'self-worth'. It is easy to get the two mixed up. What you bring to the world & what you give to those you share life with may determine how you are valued or perceived from the outside. Nevertheless, when stripped back to the base level, that which exists within you is your self-worth. Omnipresent, indiscriminate self-worth. That is you.

No number of labels or identities will change this fundamental characteristic.

There is nothing wrong with pursuing your goal/s. In fact, there are several sections in this book that advise you to do so. It is the underlying beliefs that I am addressing here. It is an important recognition that we will naturally push harder towards a goal if we are striving to get away from something. Think here of our innate fight, flight, freeze response. Whilst I am not saying that all success comes in this way, it *can* be utilized effectively, no doubt. It *can* be used to generate success in an endeavour. However, even in the case of the most 'successful' people in the world, if the underlying belief is that of not feeling good enough, or not feeling that they can be loved, the outcome will never be truly satiating... *it will never be enough.*

Making the unconscious, conscious

In IFS therapy you become familiar with the idea of your 'parts'. Your parts are essentially pieces of you, or more accurately, thoughts & feelings that have been stuffed down, supressed/repressed out of sight & out of conscious awareness (similar to Jung's concept of the shadow). Peering into the proverbial shadow allows you to revisit these memories... memories that have an emotional charge attached to them. These are the emotions we felt, our parts, that we have buried away... buried away from our awareness & buried away from the world.

Supressed & repressed though they may be, these 'parts' will subconsciously dictate your life if you do not allow them a voice from which to be heard.

As Carl Jung said, *"unless you make the unconscious conscious, it will direct your life and you will call it fate".* Ultimately, pain can be a great motivator, but it cannot bring the fulfilment & the peace that you yearn for. Try to look deeper.

The idea here is to begin to acknowledge these parts. To become aware of them & to begin to unburden them & (hopefully) befriend them.

What is it that they are, or were, attempting to do?

Were they trying to protect you?

Were they trying to keep you safe?

As noted earlier, Carl Jung developed the concept of the shadow which addresses the subconscious motivations that drive our behaviour. It can be a daunting thought to even consider exploring your shadow. Nevertheless, your shadow is still you. It is as much of you as the pleasant persona you embody in your daily interactions whilst at work or with friends.

You could begin by asking yourself why you feel uncomfortable in a particular situation or in a particular moment? Why are you having an emotional response? Why, why, why?

Eventually you will have an answer.

This practice will cultivate the skill of introspection & further your ability to self-reflect, both of which are vital for a healthy mental state.

The above are incredibly deep questions, on a deeply personal topic. The shadow is a monumental concept to comprehend, let alone to be able to integrate. As such, I will go no further in this book. I am simply providing the foundation here, the understanding & a starting point from which the therapeutic process (with a trained medical professional) can take place.

You don't see the world. You see a version of the world, constructed by your perception. Whether it be conscious or unconscious, your life's story directs the show. This means that you see the world differently to other people. It also means that what you focus on will determine what you see. Where attention goes, energy flows.

Telling a race car driver *not* to crash into the wall will have the opposite effect, actually increasing the likelihood of crashing into the wall. This is because their attention has gone from 'staying on the track' to 'avoiding the wall'. Their focus has gone from 'track', to 'wall'. What you focus on will determine what you see.

Bringing this to everyday life; if you focus on hatred & suffering, you will find it. Equally, if you focus on love & joy, you will find it. They both exist. Reality is neutral. Just like switching between radio stations, you will only get what you are tuning in to. If you are listening to rock music on one radio station, you aren't suddenly going to hear classical music no matter how hard you try. Similarly, if you are listening to classical music on one radio station, you won't hear pop music (no matter how angry & animated you become in the process).

In order to hear the other genre of music, you have to change the radio station... *you have to change the frequency.*

Each of us hold the power to change what we focus our attention on. So, I'll ask you now; which station are you tuning in to?

"The most important decision you make is to be in a good mood" – Voltaire.

Should you have found this chapter emotionally challenging or triggering, please seek out the help & support from close friends & family, as well as your GP/trained healthcare professional to help you with what you are going through. This book does <u>not</u> give recommendations or personal advice. In no way does this book, or the contents within it, constitute a working relationship, nor is it specific health or medical advice. I take no responsibility for any injury or adverse health outcome following the ideas & information in this book. For any further concerns please revisit the disclaimer at the beginning of the book.

Stress

It could be argued that chronic stress is now becoming a Western epidemic. Resulting in a vast array of negative health outcomes, from acute illness through to chronic disease, the tension we carry within our body has the potential to end our life early if not managed properly. Stress can stem from a multitude of areas, from threats arising in the external environment through to stress, tension & anxiety arising within our own psyche. Ironically, by stressing over not being stressed, you create the very stress you didn't want in the first place!
Even when undertaking health promoting activities such as exercising & working out, the physiological conditions that present themselves in the body ring the same alarm bells as that of our innate stress response, those of which could paradoxically be considered poor health markers.

During exercise, our blood pressure, heart rate & breathing rate can all increase. However, when these changes happen acutely through exercise, the damage is mitigated due to the period of rest & recovery that follows. In fact, it is during this period of rest that the body is able to adapt to the training stressors & to become more resilient to such stressors. This adaptation could be increased muscle mass when resistance training or it could be improved cardiovascular ability when training aerobically/anaerobically.
Stress, though inextricably linked with being alive, can be hugely detrimental if not managed adequately.

The 'Stress Bucket'

Imagine a large bucket in your head. On the side of the bucket is a little tap which allows what is inside to escape out when opened. This we will call 'The Stress Bucket' (48).

Each of us hold a psychological 'Stress Bucket' inside of us. The bucket may begin empty but as you progress through life it starts to slowly fill up with stressors.

For example:
The alarm clock in the morning screams out, causing you to wake in shock, far earlier than you would otherwise like to. As a result, your body is flooded with adrenaline. You enter a chaotic frenzy just to get yourself ready & out the door. You rush to arrive at work on time, encountering traffic on route, perhaps someone cuts you up on the road, maybe there are further delays due to road works.
You arrive to work (on time) & are inundated with emails & tasks that require your immediate attention. Before you know it, your bucket is now full of stressors & you have not even begun your workday!

The stressors are not limited to the workday. Some will be immediate reactions to your environment, such as those listed above, whilst others can be more long-term anxieties & concerns over the future or other issues such as illnesses, relationship troubles, financial difficulties & so on.

Ultimately, the idea of the stress bucket is to become aware of the stressors you are exposed to throughout your life, both macro & micro, within each day, week, month, year etc. As you open your mind to the situations & circumstances that result in a stress response you will begin to notice how even acute stressors can build up to a point that, if the tap isn't opened every so often, your bucket can easily overflow & wreak havoc in your life.

Many people fall into the trap of soothing or numbing themselves via substances such as drugs & alcohol in order to 'de-stress'. Whilst these behaviours may provide some temporary relief, they tend to paper over the issue & typically lead to a magnification of suffering down the line. You can't plaster over a broken leg, so to speak. Nor can you open the tap by numbing your stress or suffering. The tap only works by adopting habits & behaviours that genuinely release & reduce stress from the stress bucket. You can do this by adopting hobbies, by socialising, by partaking in leisure activities & by entertaining periods of restfulness. Meaningful interactions with those you care about, date nights, solitude & downtime can all be net positive behaviours that can help reduce the overall level of stress in your life.

Note that there will be different habits & behaviours that may decrease stress for one individual yet increase stress or anxiety for another. For example, an individual who is low in trait extraversion & low in trait openness may find it difficult & stressful to socialise or to partake in a hobby or in an environment with a group of people. Yet, this same individual may find a night spent indoors with a book or a hot bath particularly relaxing.

Conversely, an individual who is high in extraversion & high in openness may find the above to be quite unsettling & would much rather absorb themselves in the social environment of a sports team or a club, or perhaps with their friends at a pub or restaurant.

The above is not an exhaustive list & many individuals will have varying susceptibilities to stress, as well as their ability to reduce such stressors.

Think of ways in which you may be able to open the tap & allow the level of stress to reduce. As we have now ascertained, for some people this will be seeing friends, for others it can be playing a sport or working out. Some people enjoy a sauna or a massage whilst others enjoy meditation or a break from social media use – referred to, more recently, as 'social media fasting'.

Find out what works for you & begin to strike a balance, in so far that your stress bucket does not spill over uncontrollably.

Remember that not everyone will enjoy the same stress-reducing activities, nor will they have the same proclivity for down-time in general.

Referring back to the 'Big 5' personality traits that were documented in the opening chapter, & briefly re-visited above (extraversion & openness being two of the five traits), some individuals will have higher levels of neuroticism which may increase the need for leisure time &/or periods of restfulness. Others, whom may be highly extroverted & lower in neuroticism, may not require quite as much leisure time or solitude, as they tend to gain energy in more stimulating environments. This runs contrary to introverts who can find social interaction strenuous & exhausting.

Below is an example of one such 'Stress Bucket' from a recent research paper:

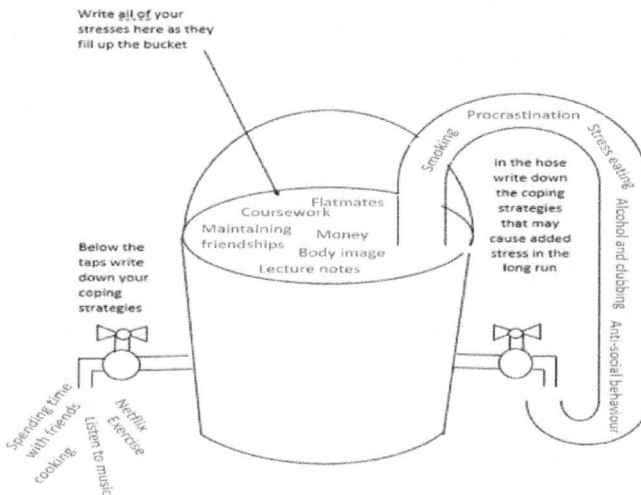

(Adapted from Williams & Powell, 2017) (49).

The practice of refining what works best for you will take time & requires a lot of introspection. Through trial & error, you will eventually find the activities (or lack thereof) that reduce the stress in your own bucket, so that you are able to turn up as best as possible in your life.
It's no good exhausting yourself & being chaotic because you think that is what you 'need' to do. This type of

behaviour, the need to people please, is something that is particularly common in people who are trying to make someone else happy, or to make someone else proud, or even as a subconscious motivation to not disappoint someone.

Whether it is the former or the latter, whoever this person is has power over you & your life. Let it go.

As we addressed in the opening chapter, there are many different areas within your life that will constitute your identity. It is worth developing a relationship between these various facets to help free you from socio-cultural influences that may be disingenuous or that simply may not apply to you.

As you begin to carve out a lifestyle that works for you & eliminate or reduce the problematic areas in your life, your stress levels will likely follow a pleasant reduction too.

Stimulus, Recovery, Adaptation

At the beginning of this chapter, we acknowledged that physical exercise & working out are also a stress on the body. There is a fantastic concept that typifies this psychophysiological effect; Hans Selye's 'GAS' (General Adaptation Syndrome).

Here, Selye suggested that the body goes through three physiological stages when faced with stress:

1) The alarm phase, where the initial shock response is identified.
2) The adaptation phase, where the individual attempts to cope with the resistance.

3) The exhaustion phase, the individual now faces the damning consequences of insufficient recovery.

In the realm of physical fitness there is a similar concept known as Stimulus, Recovery, Adaptation.
Similar to Selye's GAS, you can visualize a wave-like pattern where an individual undergoes a stressor which temporarily compromises their physical (& perhaps mental) state. This sees them fall below baseline in terms of their general health markers. Following a period of rest however, the individual will return to baseline & even end up with improved health markers, above their previous baseline.
Whether that be strength, hypertrophy or cardiovascular capability, the same applies in the arena of physical training as it does to the stressors of everyday life. Should recovery be sub-optimal, the individual will succumb to the inevitable 'exhaustion phase', as described earlier.

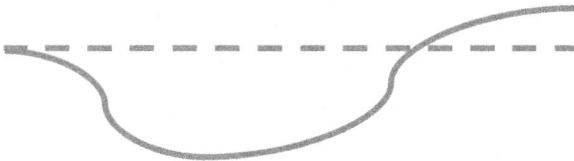

Stimulus...   Recovery...   Adaptation.

The bottom line: take time to rest!

In our modern era, where there is widespread information overload. Even those individuals who meticulously organize their environment (both physically

& virtually) to reduce their exposure to clickbait media & a degrading pop culture can find themselves falling victim to the same asphyxiating behaviour of simply consuming too much.

By consuming too much, I am not simply referring to the aforementioned pop culture & clickbait media (that which even traditional journalism is now finding itself falling victim to), but also the apparently healthy behaviours of increasing knowledge & expanding your understanding of some subject area.

We are not machines. We are not designed to be operating, let alone working, in a continuous state of stimulation & arousal throughout our entire waking day.

Prior to our current technologically advanced times there was arguably a greater propensity to take a complete psychological & physiological break during the working, or non-working, day. Typically, one would commute to work, carry out the routine activities of the working day, then commute back home to relax & unwind, care for their family & entertain themselves prior to bed. Going back even further, prior to the Industrial Revolution, the commute to a factory, or a city, for work was virtually non-existent.

Today however, in the digital era, it Is becoming incredibly difficult to detach & to switch off from work & the stresses of life. Our reluctance to power off our devices &, as such, 'power off' our anxious brains is causing a precipitous drain on our physical & mental faculties.

Practical applications to reduce stress

If we are constantly switched on, we fail to take the time necessary to ascertain a sense of presence & calm. This needs to be addressed if we want to attain peace of mind.

A helpful reframe in regard to taking on more & more information (whether useful or not) is to cultivate the practice, & the habit, of bringing your attention back to the present moment. Take a deep breath & look around... take in your environment.

What can you see?

What can you smell?

What can you feel?

If you find yourself struggling in a state of mental overload (the kind that puts us into a fight, flight, freeze response) it can be useful to focus our attention on the breath. Our breathing directly influences our physiological state. Slow breathes through the nose, with a longer exhale than inhale, can bring the body & the mind back into a state of calm, engaging the para-sympathetic nervous system. On the contrary, short, sharp, snappy breathing will tend to do the opposite – resulting in arousal & stimulation.

Furthermore, a technique known as the 'physiological sigh' can be utilized to provide some more instant feedback to the central nervous system, bringing us back to our desired state of rest & relaxation. The physiological sigh involves one long breath in through the nose, engaging the diaphragm (think belly breath), then as you get to the end of that full inhale, force yourself to take in a little more air than you would naturally, essentially creating a double-inhale of sorts. Following this extra inhale, allow for a controlled exhale either through the nose or the mouth.

This practice can be done just once or repeated a few times in order to allow the mind & the body to enter a calm, para-sympathetic state.
Professor Andrew Huberman goes into this protocol at great depth on his podcast (50) which can be found on his website or on any podcast streaming platform &, again, on his social media Instagram account (51).
*As a side note here, I would like to add that Professor Huberman entertains an enormous variety of topics via these platforms, giving out tons of free information in the realm of science, biology, neuroanatomy & psychology. I would highly recommend visiting his website &/or his social media profiles for further reading & for an abundance of educational resources on the subjects listed above.

Delving deeper into our dynamic, 24/7 work environment, if you are striving forwards in life & pursuing your goals, remain urgent with action, but do not neglect patience when it comes to the result. Life is a marathon, not a sprint. Work diligently on your craft, but do not rush.
We want to be moving forward in life, of course. This book should encourage you to do just that. In fact, it is the pursuit forward in life, in & of itself, that brings about positive emotion.

Nevertheless, rushing through life or taking on unsustainable levels of stress, particularly over a prolonged period, can be just as self-destructive as doing nothing at all. This is the idea of the 'multiplied by zero' mental model.

Essentially, this idea, noted in a podcast discussion involving modern-day thinker & the constructor of several stellar mental models, George Mack, is that; whatever you are doing, no matter what you are working on/improving upon, if that 'thing' is then undermined by a cataclysmic mishap, everything goes to zero.
During the podcast 'Modern Wisdom', Mack uses the following example: *"if you get caught, as an athlete, doing steroids... you're gone basically"* (52). Williamson, the podcast host, then adds: *"it identifies the weakest link in the chain, & no system is stronger than its weakest component"* (52).

This concept may have originated elsewhere, though the idea is conveyed well by Mack & is worthy of being included here. It should be noted that Mack also explains this concept nicely during the 'Infinite Loops' podcast, three years later, in 2023 (28). Both podcasts compliment this chapter (& this book) well &, as such, I highly recommended allocating a few hours of your time to listen to them.

Similar examples of the 'multiply by zero' could be; if you are investing or trading & the market enters a depression, or the business you are invested in goes bust. That's a zero. If you are training to get fit, or to get into a sports team, the military or the like, a catastrophic injury would also be a zero.

So, what can we take from this?

If you are loading more & more stress on yourself, whether that is psychologically or physiologically, be sure to take periods of time away from the stressors (similar to Selye's GAS model) to reduce the likelihood of encountering your own 'multiplied by zero' situation.

As we addressed earlier in this chapter, when you're in the gym, working out a muscle, what you're actually doing is breaking that muscle down. From a physiological perspective you are getting weaker... you're breaking down. It's only afterwards that you develop & grow & get stronger.

Similarly, from a psychological perspective, when you are suffering psychologically, when you are struggling emotionally & when you are breaking down, the very circumstances you find yourself in, no matter how traumatic, are providing you with the conditions to grow & become stronger.

Us humans spend so much time trying to avoid difficulty & uncomfortable situations, yet it is when we lean into discomfort that we gain the opportunity to develop. If a tree is given a perfect environment to grow & is sheltered from the outside world, it will fall over at the slightest gust of wind. It is exposure to the adverse weather conditions of wind that force a tree to become stronger & more resilient.

Penetrating deeper into the psyche, the famous psychologist Carl Jung professed that *"no tree, it is said, can reach to heaven unless its roots reach down to hell"* (53).

Methods & practices

One thing is certain in life; hard times will come for each of us. In order for us to grow & develop as a person we must subject ourselves to stress & difficulty, even failure, voluntarily. I am aware that this may sound counter-intuitive following what you have just read about the relationship between stress & human health. Nevertheless, developing your character may very well require you to expose yourself to situations & environments that generate stress. It does, however, also require the appropriate level of rest & recovery thereafter to allow for an adaptation & for personal growth.

If we are always switched on & in stressful environments, that stress bucket that we reflected on earlier will begin to overflow & will result in a cascade of negative health effects – both physiologically & psychologically. However, if we can strike a balance between stress & rest, stimulus & recovery, we can continuously develop as a human being, whilst simultaneously broadening our character & our capacity to overcome all of life's stressors.

In certain areas of the world siestas are customary periods of relaxation & rest on a given day. The adoption of siestas appear to be beneficial for health – particularly coronary mortality (54). In spite of being a culture without siestas (one, in fact, that places virtue on being busy & a 'work hard, play hard' mentality), many people are now integrating tools such as NSDR (non-sleep deep rest) or Yoga Nidra to their lives. Practices that allow for calmness & relaxation (Yoga Nidra being one such practice) tend to be associated with beneficial outcomes in both physiological & mental health (55).

Practically speaking, the idea of napping, sleeping or engaging in a Yoga Nidra practice during the daytime may be impossible for you. But could you put aside five or ten minutes somewhere during the day where you are able to remove yourself from all distractions?
Could you give yourself some time without your phone, without working, without noise or other sensory inputs? It may be easier to begin by downloading an app or with an online tutorial that guides you through a relaxation protocol, such as Yoga Nidra. Soon though, you may find yourself able to fall into periods of rest & relaxation without the added assistance... taking a complete break from life, both physically & mentally.

"You should sit in meditation for twenty minutes every day – unless you're too busy; then you should sit for an hour" - Zen proverb.

Physical health

It is very difficult to be the best version of yourself if you do not have your health. Though there do exist some circumstances in which ones' physical health may be deteriorating or otherwise compromised through illness or disease, the avoidance of physical exercise &/or physical activity can result in a precipitous decline in health, as well as our overall wellbeing.
Here we will delve deeper into what it means to be in a state of good physical health & how we can go about achieving such an outcome.

You may be expecting to see some crazy workout schedule in this chapter &, if that would serve the purpose adequately, it would be here.
Rest assured, there will be mention of what training modalities are useful & how exercise is beneficial to your health. Workout plans can, of course, be effective. However, the workout schedule & the intricacies of each particular workout are of less importance than the underlying principles of training & the habitual behaviour change that coincides with it.

Something that cannot be understated in the discussion on physical health are the beneficial outcomes for our mental health & wellbeing. Whilst I will not be penetrating the area too much in this chapter, the current evidence suggests that *"exercise is an evidence-based medicine for depression – at least as an add-on to*

antidepressants" (56). Again, this is a very nuanced area & each individual case should be treated on a one-to-one basis with a medical professional. Nevertheless, as the prevailing wisdom from the Stoic philosopher Seneca reads, "*The body should be treated more rigorously, so that it may not be disobedient to the mind*".
(We will address Seneca & the Stoics at greater depth later).

How much physical exercise should you be getting?

This will vary from person to person &, without knowing all the specific intricacies of your life, it would be impossible to give a precise answer.
The current guidelines for physical health are as follows: "*150 minutes of moderate intensity physical activity & 2 days of muscle strengthening activity*" (57).
The same recommendation can be found on the NHS website in the UK which also includes the option of 75 minutes vigorous activity as opposed to the standard 150 minutes at a moderate intensity (58).

Is this attainable for everyone? Honestly, I think it is quite unlikely...
Our busy modern lives make it extremely difficult to fit in all the physical exercise our bodies require. How is it that someone can be expected to juggle a 40/50/60 hour work week, commute to & from work, get 8 hours sleep each night, have quality family time, nurture social relationships (all of which we know to be important for our health) & be able fit the above criteria in each week?

Ultimately, your health must become a priority. If you consider your health to be important (& you absolutely should) you will prioritize it.

This is not to say that it will be easy to incorporate health promoting activities into your life. For most people there will undoubtedly be some obstacle or conundrum preventing a seamless transition into good health, whether that be some kind of health condition, a demanding job/career, familial responsibilities & so on.

If, after deconstructing your life down to the day-to-day activities, you still cannot find a sufficient window of opportunity to allocate to physical exercise, simply focus on what you can do. What is currently within our capacity, that we can do today, that is achievable? This doesn't need to be an enormous undertaking. Start small. Whatever idea you currently have, break it down into something smaller. Something is always better than nothing. Even adding in some simple changes such as taking the stairs as opposed to the escalator, walking to a shop rather than taking the car, or setting a timer every 30/60 mins to get up & move or to do some form of exercise will all begin to improve your health & wellbeing. Human beings have not evolved to be sitting down for 8/10/12 hours a day, in artificial lighting, away from friends & family. We must begin by integrating small, healthy habits – shaping our environment as best we can to allow them to perpetuate.

The targets for general physical activity (stated above) are major generalisations. They evidently pose a problem when interpreted as 'black & white' statements. You may think, "If I don't meet the criteria for five cardiovascular workouts & two resistance training workouts, I have failed & there is no point carrying on".

It's important to remember a quote from earlier on here: *"Compare yourself to who you were yesterday, not who someone else is today"* (37).

A flexible approach

If you set yourself the target of running 5km once per week or simply to go to the gym once per week (regardless of what that entails) & you do not achieve that, blanketly viewing it as a failure will inevitably cause you to suffer the downstream consequences of holding that belief.

'Black & white' or 'all or nothing', thinking is not only problematic psychologically (something we will touch upon later) but is also problematic in the sense that, whilst goals & targets are beneficial, they need to be achievable & flexible, acknowledging the fact that life will inevitably get in the way.

To combat this, we must be open to change. We must be *'like water'*, as Bruce Lee once said. Obstacles *will* appear during the pursuit of your goals. A flexible approach will always reign supreme to that of a rigid one.

Try having an 'optimal' goal & a 'non-negotiable' goal, or target. This will allow for some variance insofar that, if life throws you a giant curveball (& there will be many times that happens!) you may not hit your 'optimal' target, but you are still able to check off your 'non-negotiable' activity.

Furthermore, goals must be set relative to your specific circumstances. That means looking at where you currently are & working from there – not by comparing yourself with others.

As noted earlier, something is better than nothing. If you are currently doing no exercise at all, could you begin by taking the stairs instead of the elevator? Could you walk to the train station or the bus stop? Address one thing, no matter how small. Tell yourself you are going to do it & *then do it*. Going for a walk once a week is a step in the right direction *(pun intended)*.

Could you repeat that action for a few weeks? Perhaps then you could consider building to twice a week? Could you then add in some bodyweight exercises in the morning, at lunch, or after work?

Start small & build upon a stable foundation. Just like the construction of a house, you must build from the bottom up, bit by bit, with stable & solid foundations.

If you tell yourself you are going to do something, whether that be something physical or anything else in your life, make sure you honour your word & do it. It becomes incredibly difficult to build confidence if you cannot keep your word. Breaking the promises you make to yourself will cause you to distrust your own inner voice &, when difficult times come, your inner voice may just be all you have to depend upon.

Health across the life-span

A good example of a long-term health & fitness plan is described by Dr Peter Attia in a podcast interview with Chris Williamson (59). Dr Attia asks Williamson what he would want his life to look like in his last decade of life. He refers to this as the 'marginal decade'.

Pressing Williamson (in his early 30's himself) further, Attia asks him to describe, in detail, what metrics of health he would be seeking. Some of the examples included were to be able to walk his dog, to be able to walk upstairs & to be able to pick up his grandchildren. By working back from this final/marginal decade of life, you become able to identify what habits & behaviours need to be met in the decades prior, all the way back to the present day.

What can you do today to ensure that 'future you' gets the life he desires? Williamson, also has an all-encompassing quote that translates exceptionally well to this concept; "*what would you tomorrow want you today to do?*" (60).

When looking for something that ticks all the boxes; from hypertrophy, muscle endurance & cardiorespiratory fitness, circuit training could be your golden ticket. Gone are the unnecessary (though popular) 'Bro splits' - chest & triceps day, back & biceps day etc. These types of workouts may have a time & place but, when considering such things as time restraints, external commitments & overall return on investment, it's fair to say that these workouts are sub-optimal. They take up a lot of time &

provide negligible results in comparison to whole body workouts or 'super-setting' global movement patterns (push/pull etc).

Metabolic Conditioning

Not to be misconstrued with traditional, rudimentary exercises, circuit training really can in fact be made fun & enjoyable. A particular type of circuit training that I think is highly effective, both in terms of time, intensity & the latent health outcomes is 'Metabolic Conditioning'. Otherwise known as a METCON, this format of training has become incredibly popular in recent years thanks to an emphasis on 'functional' movement & an industry-wide popularisation of high intensity training.

To construct a METCON, you take a series of compound exercises that, ideally, utilize the entire body & group them together as if you were about to form a circuit training workout. The difference (& I would argue benefit) here is that the goal of the workout would be to complete all the exercises within a certain period of time. Alternatively, set a stopwatch & complete the entire workout in as quick of a timeframe as possible. Ultimately, it's you against the clock!
Gamifying workouts like this allows for more engagement & makes the appeal of working out more attractive. The more attractive an opportunity is, the more likely it is to become habit-forming (61).

To provide an example:
If we select five exercises, let's say;

Squat, Press up, Lunge, Chin up, Deadlift.
We could decide on doing 5 repetitions of each exercise.
Now we can choose how we are going to score the
workout... either a) set a timer & complete as many
rounds as possible within that timeframe – say
30mins/60mins etc, or b) set a stopwatch & do a certain
number of rounds – say 6/8/10 rounds, with the aim of
finishing the workout as quickly as possible.

The benefit to this type of training is not limited to the
increased level of intensity when compared to other
forms of working out. Its advantages are not limited to
the fact that it is time-efficient either. These workouts are
also infinitely scalable.
What exercises will you choose? Bodyweight or free
weights? Complex exercises such as Clean & Jerks/Power
cleans/Snatches etc, or big compound movements like
the Squat & the Deadlift? Perhaps some cardiovascular
exercises like rowing or burpees, or less neurologically
demanding exercises such as machine weights & isolation
exercises? Heavy weights or light weights? Few reps or
many reps?
Perhaps the most important variable for our busy lives;
will the workout be a 30-minute time-cap or a 20-minute
time-cap? How about just a 10-minute time-cap?
Yes, it is possible to get a great workout in only 10
minutes!

With added intensity & highly complex exercises, there
does come additional risk. You must always ensure, as
with any training, that you are moving correctly & with

good technique. Failure to do so increases the risk of injury which is something we want to avoid at all costs. With that aside, Metabolic Conditioning is a fantastic way to keep fit & healthy whilst adding a dynamic & challenging variety of workouts that are sure to keep you engaged & hungry for more.

METCONs may not be the best training stimulus for hypertrophy. However, even with traditional resistance training much of the outcome is dependent on achieving 'overload'. This typically entails taking exercises to 'technical failure' with good technique, full range of motion & graduated increases in volume. Whether growth is produced through 'Mechanical Tension' or 'Metabolic Stress', the intricacies of specific workouts are far less important than the underlying principles & drivers of muscle hypertrophy.

Intensity & 'RPE'

One of the greatest bodybuilders of all time, Dorian Yates, has proclaimed that even during his prime bodybuilding days, he was *"doing an average 45/50 minute workouts, probably four times a week"* (62). He goes on to say, *"the real sets, I call them, we're going to go to absolute failure & even beyond with forced reps, with assisted reps, maybe extra negative reps"* (62). Yates' method for training was all about taking each exercise to absolute failure. This can be incredibly motivating for people who are just getting started with resistance training or who are training around work &

other commitments, as well as aspiring bodybuilders, because it shows that you do not necessarily have to spend countless hours in the gym to achieve fantastic results.

An effective measure to obtain 'overload' is to focus each exercise of a scale of 1-10. This scale is referred to as 'RPE' (Rating of Perceived Exertion). Therefore, rather than performing 1 set of 10 repetitions at a set weight – say, 75% of your 1RM – you can now perform the same 1 set but instead aim for a RPE of 9/10.

That set you performed on one day may have reached an RPE of 9/10 at 8 reps, yet on another day it may have been at 12 reps or even at 15 reps! In this scenario if you had only taken that exercise to 10 repetitions, as it said in your rigid training plan, you would not have achieved the same level of overload that you could have done if you had factored in the Rating of Perceived Exertion scale. What you can do on one day does not accurately translate to the next. So, if you want to maximise your workouts, don't just use general loading ranges (75-85% 1RM, for example) ... integrate the RPE.

There are many variables you can manipulate in your workouts to make them more, or less, intense. The weight could be increased, the number of repetitions could be increased, the number of sets could be increased or the rest intervals between the sets could be reduced. All of these changes would increase the intensity of the exercise &, potentially, the overall session.

There are endless methods of working out in the gym. I won't be going into too much detail here as it is my belief that, as stated earlier, you can achieve fantastic results simply by following the principle of progressive overload & by utilizing the RPE scale from 1-10 – all the while tailoring your training protocol towards your specific goals.

With severe time restraints on our ability to get a high quality workout in, look no further than a 2023 study (63) which discovered that performing a 3min max burpee test was just as effective as a standard running V02 max test; meaning that in just 3 minutes, & with no equipment, you can still give yourself a fantastic workout. I'm certainly not suggesting doing 3 minutes straight of burpees – that would be torture!

The most well-known V02 max test is undoubtedly the 'Bleep Test'. Many of us will have grown up partaking in, or at least being aware of, the bleep test. Though it is debatable whether this is the most efficacious method for establishing a V02 max, it is still nonetheless a replicable method to track cardiovascular fitness across time.
An alternative V02 max test would be the 'Cooper test'. This involves a 12-minute all out run, with the aim to cover as much distance as possible.
*A V02 max test is not to be taken lightly & should be completed under professional supervision. This type of

test is used as a metric to determine your current cardiovascular ability &, as such, is incredibly strenuous.

There are a variety of ways to improve your cardiovascular health & the most common formats tend to be either steady-state exercise or interval training. Interval training can often be much more time-efficient and less mundane in its nature than that of steady-state cardio. Nevertheless, the intensity of such workouts can make them less enjoyable, particularly that of Tabata training (64). This particular study also found a general decline in enjoyment through all training modalities, with the cardio-respiratory adaptations being similar between steady-state cardio & interval training (64).

I am not going to say either interval training or steady-state training is better. You will find what works best for you through experimentation & through trial & error. Just because a training routine works for one person does not mean it will always be best for you.

Principles of physical exercise & recovery

Physical training is of paramount importance to become the best possible version of yourself. Now, don't get me wrong, you can certainly take this too far. What I am *not* saying here is that you should live in the gym, sacrifice all other aspects of your life or spend all of your money on gym clothing, dumbbells & pointless supplements. What I am saying is that you have one life & you have one body. This meat suit you exist within, this vehicle, is the only one you have. You must treat it with the respect it deserves. By doing nothing, you *are* in a state of decline.

This is particularly true as we age. Cognitive decline, sarcopenia, loss of bone density & even an increase in all-cause mortality will manifest for us all as we age. Physical activity &, in particular, resistance training will mitigate this decline (65)(66).

There are many ways to achieve positive results across all disciplines of physical training. Surf the internet & you will be bombarded with the latest new gym program to 'get a six-pack' or to 'lose body fat quickly'. Few people ever plan for the long term &, like any endeavour, for something to be truly successful it has to be a long-term commitment.
If you want to workout & exercise simply to look good, have at it! Who am I to say otherwise?
However, a house that is made of sand doesn't stay standing very long. We must address the foundations of physical training.

Let's try to base our physical appearance on something deeper – both from a physiological & a psychological perspective. Let us incorporate solid principles of *'stimulus, recovery, adaptation'* & *'progressive overload'* with regard to our training, whilst simultaneously ensuring our behaviours remain consistent no matter what life throws our way.

We referenced 'stimulus, recovery, adaptation' in the previous chapter on stress. Deriving from Hans Selye's GAS (General Adaptation Syndrome), the image below can provide the basic premise of how we can subject ourselves to some kind of suffering, some kind of difficulty &, following a period of recovery, generate a new elevated baseline.

Stimulus...   Recovery...   Adaptation.

Just like anything in life, first you must set a goal. Then you can assess whether your current actions & behaviours are taking you closer to that goal or further away.

Who you are is what you do repeatedly. Or, as James Clear put it, *"Every action you take is a vote for the type of person you wish to become"* (67).

Certain abstracts in this chapter were borrowed from my health & wellbeing book "SENSE Great Health". If you are seeking more information on physical health, exercise & training, consider purchasing a copy online from amazon.co.uk. Alternatively, check out my website www.keyworthcoaching.com for more information & resources.

Sleep

Sleep is vital for everyday functionality, not just for the avoidance of illness & disease, nor the improvement in physical health or cognitive ability, but for optimal performance in everyday life.

It is profoundly clear that sleep plays an integral role in both our physical & mental ability &, ultimately, to our sanity. Sleep is perhaps the best recovery aid known to man &, just as good sleep quality & quantity results in a number of performance enhancements spanning both the brain & body, a lack of sleep can be absolutely catastrophic.

"Lab rats deprived of sleep die within a month, and people with the rare hereditary disease fatal familial insomnia, who lose the ability to sleep, can meet the same fate within three months" (68).

By the end of this chapter you will be left in no doubt that sleep, in & of itself, is quintessential for human health.

If we look at the course of a day in terms of 24 hours, at least 8 of those hours are going to be spent at work... probably much more than that by today's standard! A further hour or two are likely to be spent commuting to & from your job. Perhaps you like to have breakfast before you leave for work which (alongside getting out of bed & ready for work) constitutes a further hour. Another hour may be spent preparing & eating dinner – that now takes us to a grand total of 12 hours.

We briefly laid out this argument earlier in the book when addressing our physical heath, but it won't hurt to address it again here.

I am all too aware that the above example is becoming rarer by the day with many of us working far more than 8 or 9 hours, with commuting times becoming longer & that (if taking the necessary care for your appearance, hygiene & health) those periods of time outside of work will also be considerably higher than stated above.
Let's say you do something to care for your physical & mental health with the limited time you have available outside of the working day; maybe you go for a walk or do some resistance training. Maybe you read a book or meet with a friend. Before you know it, we have just 7 or 8 hours remaining in which to sleep. Many of us frequently face this deleterious task.

In an attempt to mitigate some of the potential difficulty in attaining sufficient sleep, it can be helpful to allocate a sleep window into your daily structure, not to be a rigid target, but to act as a guide & assist you in maintaining your circadian rhythm & a stable sleep schedule. If this is beginning to sound a bit boring & tedious, or even over-the-top & downright ridiculous, I completely understand where you're at. Believe me, if sleep wasn't considered the number one performance enhancer on the planet, I wouldn't be emphasizing it here in this chapter!

In more recent years, there has been a movement that has seen many individuals transition to hybrid working &

working from home. This generates a potential opportunity for change. In gaining back some time, if put to good use, one would be better able to look after their physical & mental health, as well as reducing their levels of stress & their current sleep debt.

However, our newfound lifestyles are not without their downsides. For example, working from home can be socially isolating, particularly if you previously worked in a busy office or within a team. Furthermore, it can become difficult to create boundaries & differentiate between work life & home life. When you are intending to work, your environment is distracting & not fit for purpose. Following work, when attempting to switch off & unwind, it is again met with frustration due to the inability to switch off & relax.

Sleep environment

One way to help with this process is to become the architect of your own home. You must curate your home environment to make it more conducive to the desired outcome.

If you can turn one room into a home office & keep everything that is work-related in that specific area, you will likely signal to the brain that this is a space for working. Therefore, you increase the likelihood of being able to switch into 'work mode' when in this space. Following the same procedure, when organizing the rest of your house you will now regain the ability to switch off & relax in comfort & peace, just as you long for after a difficult workday.

We like to think that we are in control of our lives & that we do not require such rudimentary directions, telling our brains what to do. We are not children. We are above this, so we think.

Unfortunately for our ego we are, at the most fundamental level, simply civilised chimps. Our brains have not far evolved from our ancestors, nor our primate relatives in this regard. Without such cues from our environment, we fail to operate in a manner that is conducive to our environment.

Give each room a desired purpose. Rooms, or even areas of rooms, that are appropriately set up for their intended purpose allow the outcome to manifest without the resistance that would otherwise be present.

"Experts recommend that adults sleep between 7 and 9 hours a night" (69). However, you are not going to simply finish with the stresses of the day & magically switch off as your head hits the pillow. Therefore, it is vital that you have a pre-bed routine in place to allow for the time & space to unwind, relax & prepare both the mind & body for deep, restorative sleep.

You can find my tips & considerations for a pre-bed routine, as well as the factors that may prevent good quality sleep, in my health & wellbeing book "SENSE Great Health". The book is available online at amazon.co.uk.

The Circadian Rhythm

If there is one overriding factor when it comes to consistent, high quality sleep it is the maintenance of our Circadian Rhythm.

Human beings each have an innate 24-hour body clock. This is our Circadian Rhythm. Below, you will gain a greater understanding of its importance for human health & vitality.

Whilst we do not fully know why we require sleep, & in such vast amounts, it is clear that we have evolved to sleep during the night-time & be awake during the day. Surprisingly, there is in fact some variation in sleep/wake times across the population, with some people naturally being 'early risers' & others being 'night owls'.

In spite of this, it is overwhelmingly advantageous to keep a stable sleep/wake pattern wherever possible. We've already acknowledged how deadly (& I mean that both metaphorically & literally) a lack of sleep can be. Even subtle levels of sleep debt can lead to a myriad of problems including (though not limited to) the susceptibility of getting a cold (70) &, for the athletes out there, an increased risk of injury (71).

This sleep deprived state is exasperated today with our 24/7 model of work, a way of life that has become increasingly common in the 21st century. It is now common for individuals to work shifts & even nights on a regular basis. The impact of shift work, particularly shift work that spans the entire 24 hours of a day, cannot be understated. In October 2007, the International Agency for Research on Cancer (IARC) classified shift work with circadian disruption or chronodisruption as a probable human carcinogen (group 2A carcinogen) (72). Shift work is also associated with an increased risk of diabetes (73)(74), coronary heart disease & stroke (74).

As noted earlier, if there is one thing that may be above all necessary for human beings to improve the quality of their life, it would perhaps be this; <u>maintain a consistent circadian rhythm.</u>
Though it is not merely what you do in the evening that matters (that is if you are following the natural cycle of being awake in the day & asleep at night).
In fact, it would appear that what you do in the *beginning* of the day is also significant when it comes to ensuring a good night sleep &, by extension, a stable circadian rhythm.

A scintillating statement was made by Professor Andrew Huberman, via his Instagram channel, in which he described just how important the morning is in generating the latent effect of a good nights' sleep later that day. "*Viewing morning sunlight is right up there with those foundational practices in terms of positive impact on all the organ systems of the body & brain*".
He goes on to state; "*the yellow-blue contrast present in low-solar-angle sunlight is the optimal stimulus for your circadian system, which leads to improved wakefulness and focus during the day and improved sleep at night*".
Professor Huberman's take on a protocol for this (suggested in the same piece) is "*on bright cloudless days:*

view morning & afternoon sun for ~10min; on cloudy days: ~20min; on very overcast days ~30-60min" (75). I should note here that when Professor Huberman (& the same goes for anyone else) references the viewing of sunlight, he is not advocating for anybody to look directly at the sun or in a manner that causes strain on the eyes.

What else can inhibit good quality or quantity of sleep?

Drugs & alcohol can often be used as a tool to relax & many people use these substances in an attempt to get to sleep. The nightcap that you think helps you sleep is actually a misnomer. Alcohol is a sedative. Whilst it may help you feel relaxed & calm, it will not help you obtain high quality sleep. The use of such substances will likely result in the disruption, if not outright omission, of adequate 'Stage 4' Non-REM (deep) sleep or REM (dream state) sleep. These sleep stages are particularly important to our physiological & psychological recovery.
In fact, alcohol appears to result in an inhibited parasympathetic autonomic response & decrease in heart rate variability, both suggesting that ethanol/alcohol interferes with the restorative functions of sleep (76).

A questionnaire-based cross-sectional study involving 234 males & 159 females who had visited the general hospital found significant correlations between high AUDIT-KR (Alcohol Use Disorder Identification Test- Korean revised version) scores & subjective sleep quality, sleep duration & sleep disturbances in men (77). Alcohol can also be associated with sleep apnoea. (78).

The same applies to drugs & even sleeping pills. You cannot force yourself into high quality sleep via ingestion of such substances.

Caffeine, as wonderful a drug as it is, can prove problematic if not given the respect it deserves.
Many of us consume caffeine on a daily basis, be that a cup of coffee (or several) on the way to work, a meeting at work, a catch up with friends, right the way through to the cup of tea and biscuits on a relaxing afternoon.
You get the idea, most people enjoy tea, coffee & other caffeinated products.

Why do I say other caffeinated products?
Many beverages & food products can contain a source of caffeine (either natural or artificially induced) &, as such, many people fail to realize just how much caffeine they consume on a daily basis.
To take coffee alone; In an article by the Evening Standard in the UK, dated 1st February 2023, the following was stated; *"A medium cappuccino at Costa contains a "massive" 325mg of caffeine – around the amount contained in four cups of tea – almost five times the strength of a cappuccino from Starbucks, which contains the least at 66mg, Which? found. Cappuccinos from Greggs & Pret a Manger also contain significantly less caffeine than Costa, as 197mg & 180mg respectively"* (79).

The half-life of caffeine is of particular importance when considering sleep quality & quantity. *"The mean half-life of caffeine in plasma of healthy individuals is about 5 hours"* (80). However, caffeine does affect people differently in terms of how quickly it is metabolized due to a variety of reasons (80). There are also the potential side effects of anxiety & adverse sleep outcomes (81).

Most of us will acknowledge our chronic use of caffeine tends to drift into the afternoon. Understand that, if our last cup of coffee is consumed at 3pm, we may still have a substantial amount of caffeine in our bloodstream in the evening – a time when we want to be winding down to go to sleep. This slow process of removal means that care must be taken when ingesting coffee, tea, energy drinks & so forth later in the day.

For example, if you are planning to exercise in the evening & you usually take a pre-workout drink or a coffee beforehand, consider leaving that at home or use an alternative such as a sweetened beverage or a caffeine-free pre-workout if you must.

Whilst one individual may ingest their final drop of caffeine at midday & sleep perfectly well at night, another individual may find themselves struggling to relax & enter into deep sleep, due to a slower rate of caffeine removal.

Caffeine does, however, have a positive effect in sports & exercise performance, of which you can read more about in my health & wellbeing book, "SENSE Great Health". Again, this can be found at amazon.co.uk.

As we stated in the chapter on stress, in certain areas of the world siestas are embedded in culture to provide a customary period of relaxation & rest on a given day. The adoption of siestas appear to be beneficial for health – particularly coronary mortality (54).

Though we live in a culture without siestas (& that values business & hard work), many people are now integrating tools such as NSDR (Non Sleep Deep Rest) or Yoga Nidra to their lives. Again, as noted earlier, practices that allow for calmness & relaxation (such as Yoga Nidra) tend to be associated with beneficial outcomes in both physical & mental health (55).

What happens if we fail to achieve the level of sleep we need?

It is evident, anecdotally at least, that we become more vulnerable to stress. This is also borne out in the data...

Poor sleep damages our immune response (70) & increases risk of injury (71) as well as having detrimental effects on nutritional choices & exercise performance, as demonstrated below.

"Just two nights of restricted sleep significantly impacted hormones related to appetite & drive to eat, as well as self-reported hunger" (82).

Leptin	-18%
Grehlin	+28%
Hunger	+24%

Appetite for highly processed foods	+33 - 45%
Appetite for other foods	+23%

Human beings across the globe each follow the same stages of sleep. These universal sleep stages can be broken up into Non-REM (Stages 1/2/3/4) & REM sleep. As stated in Matthew Walker's book, 'Why We Sleep'; *"We have learned that the two stages of sleep – NREM & REM – play out in a recurring, push-pull battle for brain domination across the night"* (83).

During REM sleep the mind becomes incredibly active, almost as if awake, yet we are in an unconscious state. Brainwaves during REM sleep will be almost identical to that of a waking brain. Conversely, it is in the depths of sleep experienced in Stage 3 & 4 NREM sleep that the *"brainwave activity dramatically decelerates, perhaps just two to four waves per second: ten times slower than the fervent speed of brain activity you were expressing while awake"* (84).

Sleep stages 3 & 4 are known as slow wave sleep & are important for physical recovery. You could surmise that deep NREM sleep aids physical adaptability, whilst REM sleep aids emotional adaptability.

No matter how you look at it, sleep is the ultimate recovery tool & the ultimate performance enhancer for both our physical & mental health.

As we read in the opening of the chapter: Sleep, in & of itself, is quintessential for human health. Why we sleep though?

Well, that one will have to wait for another day!

Connection

As we have noted in previous chapters, research is now showing that social bonding & the quality of our relationships are surprisingly important for our health & wellbeing (10)(11)(12).

Many PT's, GP's & other health industry personnel have popularised the health promoting behaviours of exercising regularly, avoiding alcohol, quitting smoking &, more recently, getting sufficient sleep. Despite this, the area of social connection remains considerably underrepresented in the discussion on health. I have no doubt that this subject area will become just as prevalent in the coming years. So certain, in fact, that an entire chapter will be devoted to the topic here.

Independence is great. 'Non-neediness' (a term we will encounter later) is even better. However, our modern-day cultural shift towards individualism & egocentrism could have the nefarious result of creating considerable damage to our own health & our own psyche, before rippling out across our culture. You may have acutely witnessed this in your day-to-day life as our society becomes ever more segregated & polarized in its debate & discourse.

This book addresses you, first & foremost. Yet, what must also be addressed here is that a large indicator of your health seemingly boils down to the quality of your social relationships. Therefore, whilst the aim of this book has been to develop the best version of you possible, this should not be at the detriment of the relationships you have, or potentially could have, around you. To take it a step further, these relationships could perhaps even be considered an extension of yourself – an idea we will explore further in this chapter.

The famous biological anthropologist & evolutionary psychologist Robin Dunbar can be heard stating (in a podcast titled 'The science of making and keeping friends') the following;

"I think one of the most surprising findings that has popped out of the woodwork over the last decade, decade & a half, probably not much more than that really, in the medical literature has been the extent to which the best predictor of your psychological health & welfare, your physical health & welfare, even how long you are going to live in the future, is just the quality & number of close friendships you have… & that is way more important than all the things your friendly neighbourhood doctor usually worries about on your behalf…
All the things like how much do you eat? How much alcohol do you drink? How overweight are you? How much exercise do you take? What medicines are you on? What's the air quality in the place where you live like? All these kind of things certainly have an effect on your health & wellbeing but they are paled almost into insignificance by comparison with simply the number & quality of close friendships" (85).

Understandingly, this data has only emerged recently & may therefore take a while to flow through our culture &

create a tangible difference in our everyday lives. Nevertheless, the astonishing effects of our relationships & social engagement (or lack thereof) show us just how important it is to take care of all aspects of our health – physical, mental & emotional, nutritional, spiritual & (finally) social. Whilst many of these aspects have been explored in varying chapters of this book, it is difficult for any human to attain the heights of any health-related endeavour without taking into consideration our inherent need for social connection.

Every single human being exists in relationship to other humans, whether that is the other family members in your household, your neighbours in the house next door, the people you come in contact with at work, on your commute or (as common today) online. In this way, the human social environment that each of us are born into can be thought of as similar to that of a tree in a forest. You, the tree, find yourself within a pre-established network of other 'trees' that inhabit an area (geographic or otherwise). The complexity of such systems are present well beyond our visual capabilities. Both our social relationships & the relationships between trees operate at levels that transcend the basic human senses. Trees in a forest contain root systems that form an integrated network beneath our feet. They are not simply individual trees.

We humans operate within a social environment – even those of us who are introverted & ardently anti-social. We are not simply individual human beings. We are something more. We are inextricably interconnected to the wider social world.

Narcissism

As we spoke of in the opening chapter of the book, every human being has an inbuilt capacity for narcissism. Each of us will have felt that, at least at one point in our lives, we were the centre of attention. We all have an ego &, as a social species, we love to have that ego stroked by others.

It is important to understand this inbuilt narcissism we each hold because it is equally prevalent in those we meet. As noted earlier, some individuals possess a level of narcissism that can be deeply manipulative & damaging, yet most of us have it under control insofar that it does not intrude upon our lives, or the lives of others, in an unhealthy way.

Why am I talking about narcissism in a chapter on connection?

Firstly, it is to become aware that we all hold this capacity. We all have a yearning to be accepted & to be valued. It makes us feel good. Every species on Earth, & every system for that manner, falls into a hierarchy. Even in the dream state ideology of socialists or communists in our society, there still lies a hierarchy within such as structure – one that could, in fact, be argued to be more deleterious & oppressive than its opposition, as history would show.

If we perceive ourselves to be higher in the social hierarchy, we feel better in ourselves. We all strive to be acceptable & valued, performing tasks, achieving goals, acting in other peoples' best interests to improve our social credibility. This *can* become tyrannical &, for those who rank high in narcissism, can degenerate into one large metagame in which other human beings appear like pawns on a chessboard.

These narcissists (who would fall into the 'Dark Triad' personality types) are manipulative, vindictive types who will use other people to elevate their status within the group. For them it is all a game of superiority & deception. Watch out for these people.

For those who do not fall into this category it is important to understand that, in your interactions with others, you want to be able to see people in the same angelic light that they see themselves.

Okay, perhaps that's a stretch!

Nevertheless, when we engage with others, let's try to see the world from their perspective & to understand their point of view. This is a superb skill to hone when attempting to improve your sociability. It will elevate your interpersonal skills, the quality of your relationships & enhance your reputation as a byproduct.

Pay close attention to what people are saying to you, pick up on the non-verbal cues & engage openly with them on the topics they are discussing with you. In doing so, you show that you are listening to them & are engaged in what they are saying. This may appear trivial, but it is in fact anything but. Improving your inter-personal skills & the ability to co-operate will echo out across time & across your social interactions with others. People will respond fondly to you & will begin to value your presence.

Human beings are starving for attention, today more than ever. Show them that you are listening. Not in a manipulative way, not to selfishly advance your standing with them, but because doing so makes the person feel seen & heard.

We all want to be seen & heard.

This need to be seen, heard &, dare I say, valued can be problematic in a culture that is degenerating. Earlier in the book we spoke of victimhood & virtue. What better example of the malevolent branch of narcissism that has now permeated across our Western culture!

We are today witnessing weaponisation of (perceived) victimhood in order to generate personal gain in the socioeconomic hierarchy.

It may not appear this way on the surface, but that is because these types are deeply manipulative. To show their hand openly would cost them dearly... they are not yearning for power, they will argue. They simply want 'justice' or 'equity'. Do not fall for this play.

They want society to operate on their terms. They want control, they want power &, at the very least, they desire an elevation in their status.

To be clear, I am not *necessarily* saying that our society is degenerating & these behaviours can (& do) manifest throughout all cultures & societies. I'd like to think here that I am simply potentiating your internal alarm, as well as providing a refreshingly clear lens through which you can view these types of people & their actions, as well as our society at large without a problematic degree of naivete – a trait that these types of people depend upon for their wicked games.

Unfortunately for men today, with the current state of our culture, large portions of men are becoming invisible. It is the men who are dropping out of education (17)(18) & employment at alarming rates (18)(86)(87)(88). *"Between 1999 and 2019, the percentage of 16 to 24 year old males participating in the workforce fell 17% and that number is projected to decrease even more over the next 10 years. Other countries, like Italy, France, Spain, Sweden, and Japan, have all seen more than a five-fold increase in young men not employed"* (18). In addition, the male labour force participation has not breached 80.2% in the last 30 years. In fact, it has regularly fallen short of this figure - currently sitting at 78.1% for the year ending 2023, down from 91.4% for the period 50 years prior (88).

The impact on dating & relationships cannot be understated either. The lack of desirability most men face today is unprecedented. The above statistics certainly contribute to this, giving rise to certain sociocultural groups that hold the potential to further exacerbate such an issue. This includes, though not limited to, recent movements such as the 'Red Pill' & 'MGTOW' (Men Going Their Own Way), which we will come onto later.

This destitute road of singlehood *could* develop into a huge problem in times to come… fighting age males, perhaps the most dangerous demographic in society, are largely unseen – all the while suffering from the perpetual messaging in the media that *they* are a problem in the world.

There is an inevitability of in-fighting amongst groups of men that is prevented from escalating into violence through the use of good 'games' in society (which we touched upon earlier in the book). Yet, if men fail to integrate, or are actively restrained from engaging in the competitiveness of the market (or whatever game they choose to play) we could be treading very dangerously. Could this become a serious problem? Only time will tell. The fuel is there, like a cloud of gas building larger & denser… it only takes a spark to ignite & cause all manner of destruction.

When does a volcano turn from a tourist attraction into total devastation? *When it erupts.*

Back to the subject of connection, you don't just meet people. You meet people in a specific space & at a specific time. You didn't meet them five minutes ago when they were enjoying a nice coffee. Nor did you meet them the day after they broke up with their partner & were experiencing the raw emotion of heartbreak. You didn't meet them when they were a teenager & muddling through an identity crisis, figuring out who they are &

learning to deal with the flood of hormones that a typical teenager has to endure. No, you are meeting this individual right now... at this very place & at this very time.

Every individual you encounter has had a completely different life to you. They have had a different set of experiences, they have had a different response to these experiences, & as a result, they see the world differently to you. Rather than dismissing someone else's perspective as being 'right' or 'wrong', or 'good' or 'bad', let's begin to place ourselves in their shoes, let's get in their head & in their soul.

Thought experiment:
Standing across from eachother in a car park, two individuals are having an argument over what number is displayed on the floor of a parking bay. One adamantly testifies that it shows the number '9', whilst his counterpart proclaims it is the number '6'. You, the external observer, can see that whilst the number appears to show '9' to one person, it also shows '6' to the other. Neither party manage to see the situation from the other persons perspective & each grow angrier & more defensive until it escalates into violence.

Had either of them took the time to see the situation from the other persons' perspective they would have realised that the number on the floor was *correct for both of them* & the situation could have been resolved peacefully.

By extension, if a 3-year-old were to throw a tantrum, we understand that it is due to the fact that they are 3 years old. They want something & are unable to express what that something is. The tantrum, in this sense, can be considered a normal response. We don't turn to the child & say, *"explain yourself child, what do you want?"* (well, perhaps some people do... those who do not know any better). That response wouldn't make any sense. It would be about as effective as two people having a conversation but speaking in two completely different languages.

We understand that the child is in an emotional state & that they are expressing a need or a desire for something. We must meet that need on their terms by seeing the world through their eyes.

Don't meet emotion with emotion. That is a categoric failure on your part to see & understand the other person, whether that be a 3-year-old or a 30-year-old. Equally, you are not a 3-year-old... don't throw tantrums!

Loneliness

Today, we live in an era unlike any other. We are more connected than we have ever been as a species. The internet & the technology that surrounds it is taken for granted today. It is becoming ever more difficult to reflect on a time when we did not have instant communication with the rest of the world, despite it only being a few decades ago! In spite of this, & even in a world as connected as ours, we have worryingly high rates of loneliness & suicide (see below).

"Thirty years ago, a majority of men (55 percent) reported having at least six close friends. Today, that

number has been cut in half. Slightly more than one in four (27 percent) men have six or more close friends today. Fifteen percent of men have no close friendships at all, a fivefold increase since 1990" (89).

"In 2021, there were 5,583 suicides registered in England and Wales, equivalent to a rate of 10.7 deaths per 100,000 people". "Around three-quarters of suicides were males (4,129 deaths; 74.0%), consistent with long term trends" (90).

We now know that loneliness *"is reported to be more dangerous than smoking; high degree of loneliness precipitates suicidal ideation & para-suicide, Alzheimer's disease, & other dementia, & adversely affects the immune & cardio-vascular system. It is a generally accepted opinion that loneliness results in a decline of well-being & has an adverse effect on physical health, possibly through immunologic impairment or neuro-endocrine changes"* (12).

Suicide is multifactorial & may not simply be a result of the above points. Things are rarely that simplistic. Nevertheless, I find these statistics to be particularly concerning. The desperation & hopelessness that permeate the persona of young men today requires due consideration in the sociocultural discussion, & *not* by utilizing or weaponizing victimhood. Rather, by empowering men... by encouraging men to embrace & embody the beauty of their masculine energy & to channel this appropriately for their own benefit, as well as that of their family & society at large.

Remember what you read at the very beginning of this book; *what you do (or don't do) matters. It affects you, it affects others, it affects the world*.

Studies in the 1970's carried out by Bruce K Alexander have a painful relevance in our modern age. The seminal 'Rat Park' studies showed how rats, when given water laced with drugs such as cocaine or heroine, would continuously press a lever to deliver the drug... some of them all the way to death. However, when the rats were placed in a more natural environment, when they had gratifying social relationships & were able to play & have sex, few touched the drug filled water. Strikingly, none abused it to the point of death.

Dr Alexander also notes this potential link on his website under a segment titled 'Addiction: The View from Rat Park (2010)';
"I encounter human beings who really do not have a viable social or cultural life. They use their addictions as a way of coping with their dislocation" (91). Perhaps more poignant is the following assertion: *"the drug only becomes irresistible when the opportunity for normal social existence is destroyed"* (91).
Allow me to state that again; *"the drug only becomes irresistible when the opportunity for normal social existence is destroyed"* (91).

We do not live in the environment we have evolved for. For all our magnificence as a species, we are living in tumultuous times. Our dis-ease & dividedness (from others & from self) results in a cascade of negative downstream effects for us as individuals. This then ripples out across our society. *"The May 2021 American Perspectives Survey finds that Americans report having fewer close friendships than they once did, talking to their friends less often, and relying less on their friends for personal support"* (92).

Could it be time to prioritize your close friendships/relationships?
If they are to be as foundational to your wellbeing as we now believe them to be, perhaps it is time to devote the same level of care & attention to your relationships as you would your physical & mental health.

Early conditioning & lack of male role models
Though I do not intend to take the impetus away from what you do as an individual, I can't help but think our cultural messaging in the West (& the movement toward a feminine-orientated society) must shoulder some of the load here.
The conditioning of young boys, through institutions paid for by taxpayers' money (I'm referring to schools, universities, certain media outlets & other public sector work), can heavily influence how people think, act & behave. The conditioning we undergo in our formative years can have an enormous effect on the rest of our lives

& can greatly influence how we conduct ourselves in the world.

Within the institution of education there exists a staggering discrepancy between the number of male & female schoolteachers. This shows up in both the UK (93) & in the US (18). This, & the eye-watering level of fatherless homes in the West, are creating a vacuum in the lives of young men... one that appears to be both emotional & motional. From behavioural problems & lashing out through to a lack of viable prospects & long-term financial success, the lack of male-role models both inside the family & in the society at large, are catastrophic for young men.

The visible, overt consequence of fatherlessness can be seen in an article published by the Institute of Family Studies on 17th June 2022; *"lacking the day-to-day involvement, guidance, and positive example of their father in the home, and the financial advantages associated with having him in the household, these boys are more likely to act up, lash out, flounder in school, and fail at work as they move into adolescence and adulthood"* (94).

Perhaps the most shocking statement from the above piece is the following; *"This IFS brief reveals that America's young man problem is disproportionately concentrated among the millions of males who grew up without the benefit of a present biological father. The bottom line: both these men and the nation are paying a heavy price for the breakdown of the family"* (94).

This is not to say that women don't suffer too, either due to the absence of a biological father, or at the hands of men who themselves have not had a biological father present. Life has its fair share of suffering for each of us, regardless of who is or is not in the household. It may be the case that it is equally as damaging for girls to grow up without a biological father as it is for boys, though that is not for this book.

Where young men need a route forward in life, a path towards the highest goals if you will, a fatherless home struggles to adequately provide this. These men (of any age) are therefore unprepared to deal with life & tend to end up amplifying their suffering as a consequence. Even with a well-meaning mother in the household, the lack of a suitable male role model can leave them soft & vulnerable to the world.

Whilst I am not saying here that all mothers raise their boys to be soft, it must be acknowledged that the world is a harsh place &, as such, an overly loving mother can also be detrimental for a man's maturation. You cannot protect someone in bubblewrap & expect them to be able to take on the inevitable suffering of the world.

The nurturing mother may mean well, but by preventing chaos & suffering into the young man's life, you can also stifle potential growth.

As we acknowledged earlier, "*A harmless man is not a good man, a good man is a very, very dangerous man who has that under voluntary control*" (26).

Bad days will come… you better be prepared for them!

As we have uncovered, men will gravitate toward a group in shaping their identity – we all do to some extent, for that matter. There are 'good' groups in society & there are some 'not so good' groups, let's say.

A young man with a stable family structure & a strong biological male figure at the head of the family may navigate his way into the positive group of a sports team, a trade, a political or charitable cause etc. A young man without this, well we can see firsthand what avenues they drift into, as evidenced in the inner cities of many Western nations.

This is supported by data from the Institute for Family Studies, *"in addition to being markedly more likely to have been arrested during their teen years, young men who did not grow up with their father in the home are about twice as likely as those raised with their biological father in the household to have spent time in jail by around age 30. These association remain strong and statistically significant even after controlling for family income, race, maternal education, age, and AFQT scores"* (94).

With the latest data showing 46.3% of children in the UK being born out of wedlock (94) (though not all to single parents), I am fearful for the future of our society. This figure above has grown from 1 in 20 births in 1920. In fact, *"as late as 1978, more than 9 out of 10 babies were born to married parents"* (95).

This begs the question: where are the positive male role models? If they are not in the household, where are young men seeking them?

Extending out beyond the household, why is it that 'masculinity' can be widely demonised & casually proclaimed to be 'toxic' in many, if not all, spheres of the cultural discussion?

What is it in our current formation of society that is breeding a generation of men that appear so lonely & lost?

Whilst these are all incredibly important questions, I want to take the focus of attention away from wider society & back onto you. After all, *your* social connections & *your* relationships will never be able to satiate you if you cannot first enjoy your own company.

Take care of yourself first, then lead by example.

If you want to change the world, first change yourself. Or, as Mahatma Ghandi said, *"If we could change ourselves, the tendencies in the world would also change. As a man changes his own nature, so does the attitude of the world change towards him"* (96).

The most important relationship you will have in your life is the relationship you have with yourself. This becomes incredibly important when negotiating relationships with others, as you will come to be aware of in the following chapter.

Dating & Relationships

Our newly evolved, postmodern society has completely revolutionised the sphere of dating & relationships. I do not feel that to be an overstatement in the slightest.

We have fetishized 'love'. We have cheapened what it means to be in a committed relationship & we are, as a result, being forced to deal with the repercussions of that as a society.

The sexual marketplace of the 21st century has practically destroyed traditional monogamy. With many individuals prioritizing their job over having a family, with a trend towards cohabitation as a preferred living arrangement in the absence of marriage, & with divorce rates still markedly higher than that of the past (for those still getting married), what was once considered 'normal' for individuals & families alike is today anything but.

Despite a slight decrease in total divorces in the UK (as per the last census in 2021) the data shows a staggering increase in the levels of divorce when compared to past rates. For example, the ONS findings show that, *"The cumulative percentages of marriages ending in divorce by their 25th (silver) wedding anniversary has increased over time. For couples who married in 1963 (the first cohort with data available), 23% had divorced by their 25th anniversary. This has steadily risen to 41% for couples who married in 1996 (the latest marriage cohort to potentially reach their 25th anniversary). There have also been changes in the percentages of marriages ending in divorce by their 10th wedding anniversary over time. This* *has increased from 1 in 10 couples married in 1965 (10%) to 1 in 4 couples in 1995 (25%). For couples married more recently there has been a decrease, with 18% of marriages in 2011 ending in divorce by their 10th wedding anniversary"* (97).

Whilst women look to date up & across socioeconomic hierarchies, broadly speaking, men do not. As a result, as women continue to prioritise their careers & continue to outperform men in educational attainment (17)(18) & financial income (98), you could conclude (as stated in the last chapter) that the majority of men today are now invisible.
As a result of an increasingly global mating competition, men can no longer get by being simply 'above average'.

With progress in the workplace taking priority for many women, we are seeing huge changes in birth rates & childlessness. In fact, the latest ONS data show that *"the proportion of women who reached 30 years without a child has changed substantially over time, with half (50.1%) of the latest cohort to reach 30-years-old (born in 1990) having no children"* (99).
This does not mean that all women are remaining childless. Some are, though not necessarily by choice. Many are simply choosing to delay childbirth.
Again, this is shown in the ONS data above. *"The most common age for women born in 1975 to give birth was 31 years, an increase compared with 22 years for their mothers' generation born in 1949"* (99).

Unfortunately for many of these women, as they aspire to be workers & attain 'successful' positions in the workplace, & as the number of men in the upper echelons of socioeconomic hierarchy dwindle, it is these women who are losing the ability to attract a suitable partner. Tragically, some women fail to form a family & bear children at all.

Morgan Stanley have forecast that *"45% of prime working age women (ages 25-44) will be single by 2030 – the largest share in history – up from 41% in 2018"* (98).

Make no mistake here, I am not telling women to ditch their careers or to become housewives. Each & every person has sovereign choice over how they conduct their life & that is one of the most amazing things about our modern world. If you want to be a high-level employee in your corporation, go for it. If you want to start a business & pursue a career, knowing that it will consume every last minute of your waking day & every last bit of your energy, have at it! These are choices that you have control over but, as with any choice, there is always a trade-off. You can't do *anything* you want… & nor should you want to.

Some things will undoubtedly be more important than others. Too much choice can be debilitating, both physically & psychologically. Additionally, you likely do not know yourself as well as you could & therefore suffer the consequences of poor decision making in the process. Whilst conformity to the group is inherent in all of us, what works for one may not work for another. Keep in mind, just because some individuals may proclaim to have made the correct decision for their life & are subsequently bathing in the glory of their 'independence', 'liberation' or 'autonomy', it does not mean that they are necessarily telling the truth. The self-preservation of our ego is incredibly evident when we commit to an ideal. We hate to appear wrong, even to ourselves.

Today, men & women are both expected to work, pay taxes & live harmoniously in a society that makes such work a necessity in order to bring about the latter. A single income is rarely sufficient today & the outcome, I fear, could result in the degradation of the family. Why do I say this?
If both parents are out of the house, working excessive hours & struggling to make ends meet (as many do), how can a harmonious home-life persist?
Even with the prioritization of the family & the relationship, the divorce rate would appear to speak for itself in this regard.

If a man or woman wants to work & meticulously plans out their life (so as to make it a noble & achievable pursuit) whilst not causing detriment to their relationship or their family, then who am I to say any different. However, what works for one person may not translate to the next. To pedestalize work above all else, at the potential expense of the things that would appear to matter the most (family, close intimate relationships, a strong social support network) may not be the highest virtue for all to aspire to.

Socio-cultural depictions & sex differences
Western culture has evidently undergone a movement toward feminism & fem-centric ideals, whilst simultaneously deluding the public consciousness into believing men & women are the same & that there are no differences in what men & women a) can do, or b) want to do. This area of discussion tends to be emotionally charged in our public discussion today so I will try to tread carefully here.

How are men portrayed in the socio-cultural discussion. Are they ever spoken of in a positive manner? Are they ever recognized for the vital duties they perform in the world, both inside the family unit & in the broader society at scale?
No... it is just expected, or at least trivialized.
In most cases it is simply ignored. If men are praised at all today it is for their embodiment of feminine attributes, or of supporting their wife or partner.
Whilst I do agree that it is important for men to develop soft skills & emotional awareness, we are fundamentally built to endure. Men are disposable in a way that women are not. Existence in a safe society, with security & abundance, is not necessarily conducive to building strong men... & when tough times come, you want strong men.

Men operate, both physically & mentally, with a magnitude of difference from that of females. Jung spoke of the 'anima' & 'animus' – the dormant aspects of femininity within the masculine &, equally, the dormant aspects of masculinity within the feminine; similar to the Taoist concept of 'Yin and Yang', the dualism that exists in all things.

Nurturing these aspects can of course be beneficial. However, elimination or cultural repression of our natural masculinity is neither beneficial for men, women, or society at large.

This is not to say women don't play a vital role in the world, nor is it to say that they have life easy. Not at all. It is to point out the huge discrepancy in respect & gratitude toward those who sacrifice their life (yes, in many cases, sacrifice their life) in return for the bitter hand of 'misogyny' to slap them across the face. If it is deemed misogynistic to tell men to take responsibility, to do what is required, to protect & provide, & to be better men then so be it. That says more about the culture than it does about the book you are reading.

Men are desperate for a word of encouragement, for someone to turn to them & say "I see you" or "I respect you". Yet, for you to be seen or respected you must first be an honourable individual. If you do not conduct yourself with integrity & honesty, if you do not work hard each & every day to become a better person, if you do not act in service to something greater than yourself, why would you be deserving of such respect?

Many people who take ideological positions in a debate around the cultural messaging of masculinity & femininity fail to realise that men & women work best together. Our natural, biological predispositions & temperaments *can* come together to be beneficial for the family, beneficial for the relationship, & beneficial for the society as a whole. It serves men, women & society best to have strong men around. Strong men protect. Strong men act ethically.

As mentioned earlier in the book, "*A harmless man is not a good man, a good man is a very, very dangerous man who has that under voluntary control*" (26).

If you think strong men are bad, wait until you see what weak men will do.

In our current, Postmodern society everything gets boiled down to the group identity. In such a case, history shows us that whichever group feels weaker or lower in the social hierarchy will be chomping at the bit for the opportunity to take down the superior group. You may be able to notice certain 'groups' like this in our society today – those who use a social cause or specific characteristic to initiate change & to elevate their position in society.

It is not my intention here to say that women are inferior to men, that is categorically not what I am saying.

In fact, it is weak men who feel powerless, & when you give weak men power (the sense of power that they yearn for) they will use it malevolently to cause all kind of mayhem & destruction.

Men & women are not the same. You know things are getting crazy when you have to state something as obvious & foundational as that!

There are biological differences between the sexes when it comes to testosterone & strength, as well as bone structure & perhaps even genetic predispositions to certain traits & behaviours, disagreeableness being perhaps the most obvious (100). Additionally, men & women differ in the types of work they enjoy &/or pursue. This, despite movements in recent times to coerce women into STEM fields, appears to be evident cross-culturally.

Finally, by the time women enter the period of life where their fertility & sexual market value is beginning to decline (to put it very matter of fact) they tend to shift their desire away from work & towards settling down & raising a family. This can be seen in the ONS data (stated earlier) which shows us that it is now most common for women to have children at 31 years (with more women childless at 30 years-old than those with children for the first time since records began) as opposed to the much younger age of 22 years in the past (99).

This transitional period is completely understandable. In fact, it is one that you could argue is inevitable for individuals of both sexes. Peoples' values change as they get older, as do their priorities & what they find attractive. Yet, as the statistics & projections showed us earlier, this process is not quite as seamless as one would wish.

Modern dating

If women date up & across the socio-economic hierarchy for an ever-dwindling group of men, why don't these 'high value' men choose them?

Firstly, male attraction & female attraction do not work in unison. What women value in men is not what men value in women. Also concerning is the fact that the generation of men & women born into the digital era are now recognizing the (largely subconscious) dual dating strategy people possess.

In today's media age we are readily presented with the movement of individuals back & forth between short-term dating strategies & to then appeal to a long-term partner afterwards. Some individuals are considered a good fit for short term mating, whilst others are a suitable fit for long-term provisioning.

Thanks to the 'swipe-right' dating economy & our widely connected, transparent social media age, the behaviours of both men & women are now largely observable & increasingly predictable *(& they aren't so flattering either)*.

This 'swipe right' social dynamic (alluded to above) that we now find ourselves embedded in through dating apps & the 'likes/DM's' environment presented by social media creates a level of intrasexual competition that has never been seen before. You now have a huge discrepancy in the dating sphere where it is often said that 80% of the women are seeking out the top 20% of men. (I must say that figure appears to be very generous!)

Meanwhile, the remaining 80% of men are left to battle it out for the other 20% of women.

This type of inequity is visible in Pew Research Center data where the following is stated; *"54% of women say they have felt overwhelmed by the number of messages they received on dating sites or apps in the past year, while just a quarter of men say the same. By contrast, 64% of men say they have felt insecure because of the lack of messages they received, while four-in-ten women say the same"* (101).

This could prove troublesome for both men & women. Which brings me on to my next point; why will these men (who are high in socioeconomic status or otherwise highly attractive to women) not settle down with one particular woman?

The men who are in this top bracket (of ~20%) have all the options. They have ample access to the majority of women, all at their fingertips. Since the dawn of time, this proposition would result in the man of choice taking full advantage of the situation at hand, spreading his genetic material freely & indiscriminately. An evolved, biological response like that will take some overcoming. Whilst it is common for men to complain of this wild discrepancy found in the dating market today, ask yourself honestly; if this were you, would you settle down with just one female?

Unfortunately, this dating dynamic disrupts the wider culture when espoused online & through the media. Women see *all* men as being 'players' or 'narcissists' that

use women for their own pleasure & have 'commitment issues'. Is this true? Of course not. However, as noted above, the majority of men are invisible to women. Ultimately, most men live hopelessly sexless lives. Meanwhile, most women get used by the men whom they perceive as being of particularly high status.
I am certainly not advocating any of this. I am simply bringing it to light.

If past generations inhabited a staunchly religious environment, with strict rules around promiscuity & infidelity, the modern dating culture & social landscape has taken on a complete reversal. This reversal appears to be causing significant problems for men & women alike. Departure from the past may appear beneficial on the surface, & whilst society must always evolve & move with the times, complete disregard of the norms & values that guided the lives of generations before us may in fact pose greater detriment in the long run.
It would appear that tradition is likely the answer to a question, or a set of questions. Under such a premise, 'tradition' could be loosely translated to 'solution'. Whilst society is always moving & never stands still, discarding tradition altogether does not appear to be serving us (both at an individual level & as a society) with a promising vision for the future.

We appear today to be living in a culture of mistrust & deception, narcissism & self-centred indulgence. The only thing that is in your control is what you do. Take the necessary steps to make yourself the kind of person who could be desirable to women (or to men if that is your preference).

Take an aggressive but honest assessment of your life. Whether you like it or not, this is the point from which you are starting from. I'll say it again; men can no longer get by being simply 'above average'.

You may recall in the opening chapter of the book we spoke about the different parts of your identity & how a well-balanced life will incorporate relationships – both through friends &, hopefully, an intimate partner. Whilst undoubtedly important to a well-rounded life, putting dating & women at the top of your value hierarchy can be just as problematic as the dating environment itself.

Take a moment to ask yourself: Does this sound like a healthy long-term strategy for my life?

Building upon this point, podcast host Chris Williamson has formulated a fantastic concept around the issue of what it is 'you' value, verses that which society has conditioned you to value.

Following a discussion he had with Joe Rogan, Williamson (who can be found across all social media sites under the title '@ChrisWillx') termed it 'Rogan's Difficulty and Value Conflation':

"... "Look at the car he's driving, look at the watch he's wearing, look at the girl he's with. That's unattainable to many people, so it seems valuable. But when you attain it you realise that it's not valuable, it's just difficult to get"" (102).

They look like they have value, yet they were actually just difficult to get.

I am not advocating for men to date non-exclusively per-se. Nor am I advocating for some ultra red-pill, MGTOW (men going their own way) movement. Neither will I pretend that traditional relationships & strict obedience to gender roles & social customs are without problems of their own. You do not need to pick a side here. Try to avoid the natural inclination to dig your heels in or to lean into any preconceived biases. Acknowledge your own potential to take a tribal viewpoint on such topics & take a moment to detach from any subjective interpretation.

Understanding the dynamics of dating, as well as the larger cultural influences at play, is necessary for any satisfaction in the realm of relationships. Recognising the current framework from which you are operating within socially (a globalised sexual marketplace & a 'swipe right' dating economy) will allow you to navigate your way in today's dating world without being blindfolded to reality. Yet, as stated above, the most important thing is perhaps distinguishing between what society says you should want & should value, verses what you personally value.

Who is #1?

To re-iterate, the most important relationship you will have in your life is the relationship you have with yourself. You first, always. Though this appears selfish on the surface, it is actually anything but.

We have been conditioned to look for love outside of ourselves to find 'the one', or our 'other half'. Our culture propagates this myth through TV, film & other media. Whilst there is nothing wrong with forming healthy relationships with others, whether that be through friendships or intimate relationships, they can only be truly developed once a healthy relationship is established with yourself.

You will never find a relationship with just one unhealthy person in it. Why? Because a healthy person would not allow themselves to enter a relationship with someone who is not healthy themselves, knowing all too well that the relationship will be problematic, if not outright toxic, with such an individual.

Two halves might make a whole but, let it be perfectly clear, if you are not whole yourself, you are not ready for an intimate, long-term relationship.

Did you feel a push back from your conscience when you heard the statement 'you first'?

Take a look at your life. Do you feel as though you have been serving other people & have been a 'good' person, offering yourself up with a smile & grace? Now, do you treat yourself with the same kindness, care & compassion? Perhaps you are quite an agreeable person & you fear upsetting the applecart or rocking the boat, so to speak.

The reason it appears selfish to put 'you first' if because, for most of your life, you have likely been told or conditioned (consciously or otherwise) to put somebody else first. It could have been your mother, your father, your sibling, a friend or an intimate partner. You serve up the best version of yourself in the hope of love & acceptance from the world but, more often than not, you are left feeling unfulfilled & unsatisfied.

It should go without saying; always nurture the relationships you have around you. You want to be the friend that others can turn to in times of suffering. You want to be the man who holds himself in high regard & therefore receives the same level of respect from others. You want to be the man who encourages the betterment of those around him & simultaneously celebrates their successes as if they are your own. You want to be strong enough to be depended upon. You want to be the man that can protect & provide, both for you & for your loved ones. Yet, at the most fundamental level, you also want to *"Treat yourself like someone you are responsible for helping"* (103).

Loving yourself is a selfless act which will be beneficial to those around you just as much as it will benefit yourself. When you are content & fulfilled, when you are whole in & of yourself, you can put your best foot forward in the world.
This does not mean that you hide away from the world 'loving' yourself until you feel ready to re-enter society. What it means is actively designating time in your day where you prioritize yourself. It is when you put yourself first. It is when you gain the ability to say "no", *& to mean it.* In doing so you are telling yourself that you matter & that you are willing to provide yourself with the

attention, care & love that you would otherwise seek from others. You no longer need to find or receive love from the world because you are meeting that need yourself. You are giving yourself permission to feel that love, without guilt & with full acceptance of who you are.

If you aren't consciously reinforcing the message of being worthy of love, it will always evade you. Somebody else may be able to show you love, whether that is through an intimate relationship, friendship or familial relation, yet it will never truly make you feel whole. *You* have to believe it first & foremost.
Stop hoping for somebody else to complete you. It is only you that can do that. If you don't love & respect yourself, why would anyone else?

This isn't something that will magically occur overnight. Most of us have grown up in a culture that conditions us to seek comfort & love from our external environment, rather than cultivating it within ourselves.
Furthermore, it thrives on our insecurities, driving consumption of a whole manner of goods & services. This is not to say that there is anything wrong with making an effort & spending time & money on others. In fact, you probably should invest in your immediate relationships (generosity it a great attribute to have). However, you cannot buy love. Desire & arousal are either there or they are not. Further, intimate relationships tend to have relatively little to do with financial affairs as they do with shared experiences & a

deep bonding that penetrates the superficial layers of being.

Nevertheless, you will find every person is different in terms of how they love, what they find attractive, & what they don't. This is due to many reasons. Of course, some general behaviours such as poor hygiene & a permanent negative mood will be universally unattractive. Yet certain behaviours & personalities can be attractive to one person whilst being unattractive to another. This is going to result from an individuals' lived experience, particularly their childhood.

Referring back to the chapter on connection, if we are unable to see the world through the other persons' eyes, we will fail to understand how or why something is deemed attractive/unattractive to them.

Whilst I will not give you some cliché spill of "just be yourself", I believe British comedian Jimmy Carr sums this up well when he states, "*People either want tea or coffee; what no one wants is a weird mix of the two*" (104).

Lastly, & perhaps most importantly, certain actions, behaviours & personality traits can sometimes demonstrate an underlying sense of neediness.

Neediness is parasitic. It is a repellent. Nothing is as anti-seductive as neediness. When your attention is focused on those outside of yourself, at the detriment of you & your own wellbeing, others will sense it a mile away. To women this is perhaps the most volatile turn-off found in a man. To men, this is a preposterous display of weakness & vulnerability.

Do not mistaken this for some kind of 'man up/toughen up' speech. You do not have to be the hardest/toughest man in the room – the man without a chink in his armour. However, you do need to have love & respect for yourself. Failure to do so could be catastrophic.

It is your responsibility to feel love. You owe it to yourself. Your relationship with yourself is the most important relationship you will ever have. Nourish it at every opportunity.

Stoicism in the Postmodern Age

As Seneca, one of the most notable of the late Stoics, recounts; *"We suffer more in imagination than in reality"*.

It is often noted that the books, texts & lessons that have survived over extensive periods of time are likely to hold the wisdom we require to progress through our lives today. Merging the wisdom from age-old traditions & philosophy with modern day schools of thought, this chapter seeks to bring the old & new together in a unifying light, one to guide & shape our mental aptitude. It is not intended to be some new age epiphany. It will, however, aim to utilize wisdom from both the past & the present to generate a new worldview & perhaps a new, reformed perception of self.
This is ancient philosophy, applied to our modern environment.

Buildings upon Seneca's statement (above), bad days will come... that is incontrovertible. But why waste a perfectly good day worrying about it?
Take a moment. The world is still turning. Whatever is done, is done. As expertly communicated through the modern modus operandi of the 21st century (social media), 'The Mind Architect' Peter Crone states; *"What happened happened, and it couldn't have happened any other way... because it didn't"* (105).

All of our 'problems' live in our head. They exist within us. Just as Epictetus acknowledged, *"People are not disturbed by things, but by the views they take of them"*. Our problems manifest under our own permission. This is a bitter pill to swallow. No one wants to come to the understanding that it is in fact ourselves who are responsible for what we are feeling.

Bring awareness to what it is you are perceiving as a problem. Ask yourself whether it is objectively true or whether it is simply the lens through which you are peering through.

It is our perception that determines our reality.

Of particular relevance here is a quote you read earlier in this book; *"Nothing is good or bad, but thinking makes it so"* - Hamlet, William Shakespeare.

Taking responsibility for your suffering is no small feat. However, the wisdom in this chapter (as well as the rest of the book) will hopefully create the foundations, the building blocks if you will, from which you can carve out a path forward in life for the benefit of yourself & those around you.

The chance of you even existing, let alone existing in a world as advanced as those in the West, in a country where you have food & shelter, is so astronomically miniscule. Your parents had to have sex at that exact moment that they did for you to have been created. The same thing had to happen for their parents & their parents too, recurring right the way back to the dawn of time. If the timing was slightly off, if just one variable of an almost infinite number of variables was slightly changed, you would not be here today. You certainly would not be reading this. Both my & your ancestors had to endure the brutality of everyday life, both through the ruthless destruction of natural disasters, illness & disease, & through the unforgiving societal structures that presented a torrid affair of conflict, war & death.

Prior to our modern comforts, these struggles were confronted in one way or another on virtually a daily basis. Fighting for survival during some of the darkest periods of our evolutionary past, each of our ancestors resisted some of the most disastrous circumstances in order to survive & reproduce. Their actions allowed you to be here today, for you to exist on Earth at a time when there is drinkable tap water, an abundance of food from across the globe, international transportation & a web of wireless interconnectivity linking one side of the world to another. If you are here today & able to read this book, you are in an incredibly fortunate position.

Our unique existence
Though not an ancient Stoic, I absolutely love Professor Brian Cox's philosophy regarding our species & on what it means to be alive. It deserves a place here, in this section of the book. Cox explains:
"the earth is one planet, around one star, amongst 400 billion stars, in one galaxy, amongst two trillion galaxies, in a small patch of the universe... so we're indefinitely small. But if you think about what we are, we're just collections of atoms, some of them are as old as time &

some of them, the other ones, were made in stars… so we're all cooked over billions of years & we're in this pattern that can think. So suddenly, you have a means by which the universe understands & explores itself, which is us… & that sounds unlikely that you can have a few things that were cooked in the hearts of stars, you stick them together into patterns & suddenly it has some ideas & starts writing music & art" (106).

The famous author Robert Greene also has a fascinating take, one that is not dissimilar to Cox's, which he relays in a conversation with Chris Williamson on the 'Modern Wisdom' podcast. Greene states the following:
"…you go through the 70,000 generations of people prior to your being born. Think of how odd is was that your two parents met, how unlikely it was. Multiply that by 70,000 going back all the way to your ultimate, first ancestor. So you being alive, you having two legs, two arms & a brain, is so astronomically unlikely. So just think of that every day. Think of how small, think of how insane it is just to be alive" (107).

I'd encourage you to re-read those two passages a few times to really let the magnificence of existence sink in. Still feel like squandering what precious time you have left here?
Many of us go through life with our heads down – focussed, disciplined, industrious. We are on our purpose, striving forward. Though advantageous, at times it can be a great practice to stop & appreciate existence.

To be clear, I am not saying stop being productive, nor am I saying to stop developing & refining who you are & what you do. I am simply saying that it may be worthwhile to take a moment or two to show gratitude for life.

Having a gratitude practice may not solve all of your issues, but taking a moment each day to put life into perspective can be extremely beneficial.
I am not talking about reflection solely on 'your' life. I am not talking about reflection on just 'your' particular set of circumstances.
Take a moment to take in *Life*.
This experience is far greater than you or I & it's about time we showed some appreciation for that.

We shape our reality

You may not like it but, as articulated earlier, the troubles & problems that exist in the world actually exist in your head. Few people ever get to a level of introspection whereby they can detach from the outside world & acknowledge that the world they perceive each day actually exists within them. It is a projection. As the phenomenal author, comedian & political commentator Konstantin Kisin stated on the 'Modern Wisdom' podcast, *"perception is projection"*… *"you see what you expect to see, you perceive your own projections of the world"* (19).

We know this to be true, loosely speaking. If I were to put something specific into your conscious awareness, such as a certain shop or restaurant or a certain colour car or designer brand, I can predict with a fair degree of certainty that this specific 'thing' would begin to crop up more frequently in your field of vision. Whatever is in this underlying (& perhaps unconscious) net of perception, we are likely to see manifest. Sometimes this is conscious, sometimes it is unconscious. Either way it will pay great dividend to become aware of this.

Our thoughts, feelings & emotions live within us &, as proclaimed by Marcus Aurelius, *"your soul takes on the colour of your thoughts"*.

The internal dialogue will shape the external reality.

That is not to say that there are not calamitous events in the world that leave behind a wave of destruction. A tsunami or a hurricane will show you that, as will the atrocities of genocide & war – just look at the bloodbath of human history! It is also not to say that there aren't people who are capable of inflicting severe harm on others for no reason other than their own sick sense of pleasure; look no further than those who embody narcissistic, psychopathic, Machiavellian (the dark triad) personality traits.

Understanding this is vitally important. If we walk naively through life believing all is well & that certain individuals will not harm us or wrong us, we put both ourselves & others at risk of being manipulated, hurt & taken advantage of.

Nevertheless, it is a humble recognition to acknowledge that, in this world, if there is *no you* then there is *no problem*. Reality is neutral. Whilst you may encounter an obstacle in life & suffer the inevitable doubt & anxiety that rises as a result, without you the problem disappears altogether.

Previous chapters have demonstrated that we can still formulate a plan & we can still have a direction & a positive route forward in life. Yet, ultimately, we must have humble acceptance of the fact that, without us, the world does go on.

As stated earlier in this chapter, this experience is far greater than you or I. As such, let's allow life to flow through us, rather than trying to control & direct it ourselves.

"Don't row… sail" – myself, Jack Keyworth.

Modern day writer, marketer & entrepreneur, George Mack, has a fantastic concept regarding how our thoughts, feelings & actions interrelate to one another. Many of us will be aware of 'top-down' processing & the logical stages of *'thinking – feeling – acting'*. Yet, in order to change how we think or feel, Mack states the following: *"How you feel impacts how you think & act, how you act impacts how you think & feel, & how you think impacts how you feel & act"* (108).

FEEL	ACT	THINK
THINK ACT	THINK FEEL	FEEL ACT

Following Mack's analysis, we could conclude that for our mood to change (or more precisely our thoughts & feelings) it may be more advantageous to begin with action. If we can get ourselves into a different state of being by 'doing' something, then we can benefit from the downstream effects of changing the way we think & feel. Struggling to think your way out of a feeling problem? Lead with action.

At a biological level, our brain perceives the external environment through the senses. This sensory awareness culminates in the release of afferent neurons, sending information through the central nervous system (CNS) & to the brain. Following this we have a release of efferent neurons, creating a response in both our autonomic 'state' (being either sympathetic or parasympathetic) & in physical action (relaxation or fight/flight/freeze).
All of this occurs at a rapid & almost incomprehensible rate. We aren't always consciously aware of this, yet we sure as hell feel it when sudden circumstances disrupt our routine day-to-day activities.
We can infer from this process a quote that is widely attributed to the late Victor Frankl; "*Between stimulus & response there is a space. In that space is our power to choose our response*".

Our suffering lies in the narrative *we* have created around the 'thing'. But rest assured, if there is no you then there is no problem. It is important to understand that we cannot control life. Nor can we control what happens to us... we can't even control when our heart stops beating!

We assume that our thoughts & feelings are because of an event or a wrongdoing or something that is happening to, or around us. This is simply not the case. It is our response that creates our suffering.

In any case, this is actually the favourable condition. If we are to acknowledge that it is ourselves who are creating our stress & our suffering, then it is also within our own capability to change this.

The ABC of life

I have a mental model that I call *"Jack Keyworth's ABC of life"* – because that doesn't sound at all grandiose! The model encompasses the following three areas: *'Acceptance', 'Benevolence'* & *'Curiosity'*.

I term it as such because our alphabet/ABC is the foundation upon which the language we speak, write & communicate with depends upon. It is the absolute foundation from which social relationships, culture & civilisations are established & maintained. Without something as fundamental as language underpinning our society, we cannot communicate & co-operate effectively... we descend into chaos & risk civilisation breakdown.

At a psychological level, indeed for our psychological wellbeing, we must see things as they are, rather than as we want them to be. My ABC mental model seeks to cover the three foundational principles for a positive relationship between yourself & the world, integrating both the past, the present & the future.

JACK'S ABC'S OF LIFE:
- *ACCEPTANCE*
- *BENEVOLENCE*
- *CURIOSITY*

Beginning with 'Acceptance', can we acknowledge what is happening around us... perhaps even to us? Can we be okay with these circumstances as they appear?
Failure to accept 'what is', to accept life on its terms, will cause resistance & suffering – practically by definition.
Your life has unfolded the way that it has & the world is the way that it is. Wishing for something different is futile & fails to change anything.
You have the choice over how you feel about things, both internal & external. Life may not be perfect, & your life may in fact require a profound overhaul, but without acceptance (that is acceptance of the world & of yourself, of the past & of the present) you cannot be at peace.
Therefore, just as the alphabet begins with 'A'; my 'ABC' begins with 'Acceptance'.

Following onto 'Benevolence' it is important, perhaps even vital, that we address the world with the honest intention of 'being good' & 'doing good'. Just like a dropping a stone into a pond of water, what you do ripples out to those around you & to the wider society. As we have now established, we are all connected – to all people & to all things, to some degree at least. Even if it is just on the basis that you share the same land or the same Nation State, you want to operate & co-ordinate yourself honestly & with the intention of doing good in the world.

Jordan Peterson noted in his book '12 rules for life', "*Tell the truth - or, at least, don't lie*" (109). You cannot tell a lie without lying to yourself. This causes you harm as you blur the lines of reality & can no longer trust yourself. Political prisoner & author of 'The Gulag Archipelago', Aleksandr Solzhenitsyn holds one of the most disturbing declarations in this regard when he claims that "*the line separating good and evil passes not through states, nor between classes, nor between political parties either – but right through every human heart*" (110).
Aim to do good.

Finally, 'Curiosity'. As we make our way through the uncertainty of life it can be easy to fall into the trap of anxiety, trying to control outside events & assert some level of order to generate a state of calm & comfort at a psychological level. We humans tend to seek predictability & err to the side of caution for our protection & safety. This is how we have evolved as a species & it has certainly served us well throughout our evolutionary journey. The point I am making here is not to fight this natural impulse, not to tussle & resist the fact that each of us possess a craving for safety & security (refer back to 'A' – 'Acceptance').
Rather, it is to acknowledge the feeling of unease that coincides with anxiety & to sit with it. Connect to the energy, even if it is difficult, & utilise it as best you can.

A perpetual state of anxiety can be debilitating & is certainly not what I am advocating for here. Nevertheless, there is nothing inherently wrong with the feeling of anxiety. Life *is* dangerous after all.

If we were to shut ourselves off from anxiety provoking situations, we would seldom reap the rewards of overcoming our feats. We would lack courage & would fail to develop into the best version of ourselves.

As Chris Wiliamson recounts, *"the magic you are searching for is in the work you are* avoiding" (111).

In the chaos of life lives opportunity. I am by no means suggesting you throw yourself into chaos but, as the former Prime Minister of England, Benjamin Disraeli recounted, *"the secret of success in life is for a man to be ready for his opportunity when it comes"*.

As we progress through our life, let's keep an eye out to find the opportunities that we may otherwise miss in the safety of comfort & predictability.

"A ship is safe in a harbor, but that is not what ships are for" (112).

Stay curious.

If it were not the case that our suffering lives within us, it would mean we have no ability to change it. What a hopeless situation. If the world is doomed & our lives meaningless (& we know it) then why would anybody carry on?

Unfortunately, the cultural narrative that has been propagated over the better part of a generation now has been exactly that... the world is doomed, we are in a climate emergency &, even if we abide by everything we are told, we are still unlikely to make amends for the destruction our forefathers & humankind have caused. Perhaps before we lecture the world, we should adopt responsibility for our own lives in the present. As such, even if the above was a categorical truth, we could (dare I say should) reflect once again on inspiration from Mahatma Gandhi; *"If we could change ourselves, the tendencies in the world would also change. As a man changes his own nature, so does the attitude of the world change towards him"* (96).

The fact that we are able to change the way we perceive the world means that the power lies within us. It is up to us to change. No longer will we wave the victim card when life's inevitable suffering manifests itself. We can now take ourselves away from trying to control & influence the world, to make it the way that we want, or need, it to be. We *can* be okay, regardless of what happens around us.

Momento mori... remember that you will die. You have one go at this & the clock is ticking.

Journalling

It's becoming ever more popular (dare I say, even trendy) to have a journalling practice. Personally, I think journalling is a fantastic habit to cultivate. Whilst you could use a journal practice to develop ideas & strategies to improve your life or to take actionable steps forward (all of which are beneficial), a journal is much more than a list of things to do, or actions to complete.

Journalling allows us to empty our brain of our thoughts & feelings. It doesn't have to be perfect. It doesn't need to lead to anything. In fact, it doesn't even need to make sense! There are no fixed rules with journalling &, as a result, there is less likelihood of falling into the 'paralysis by analysis' that is so common in people today. This cognitive 'hiccup' originates in our perfectionist tendencies. As we recognized earlier in the book; *"Perfectionism is procrastination masquerading as quality control"* (47).
There is no 'perfect' practice here, simply 'brain-dump' onto the page.

A lot of what comes out may seem nonsensical, that is fine. In fact, to begin with you may find yourself stumped, finding yourself sat there with a pen in your hand, staring at the blank page. That is okay.
Keep the journal present, perhaps at your bedside, & open it every evening or so, before you go to bed. When the time is right, something will come up. Void of distractions, allow your thoughts to manifest onto the page. These thoughts have their own creative desires… release the impulse to control them & let them run free. This needn't be a rigid practice, nor do you have to write something. The magic in journalling is that no matter what gets written onto the page, it takes that weight, that emotional load, out of you.

You may remember, in an earlier chapter we spoke of the shadow & of making the unconscious conscious (the actual quote was, *"unless you make the unconscious conscious, it will direct your life and you will call it fate"* – Carl Jung.

Through the practice of journalling, that which is inside you (whether you are aware of it or not) can make itself known. It releases the weight of the load that lives within your psyche & your soul. If there is one thing that will undoubtedly benefit your life it is this: <u>Start journalling.</u>

To bring this chapter into everyday application, I feel that the following quote from Naval Ravikant is pertinent; *"I picked an hourly rate for myself… & I said I'm never going to squander my time for less than this. Originally it was $500 an hour, then I upgraded to $5000 an hour. Pick an aspirational hourly rate"* (113).

This is a useful way to live your life in accordance with your values & to begin valuing your time – literally! Most of us live to work rather than work to live. This practice may just change that.

Regardless of how your life is currently laid out; whether you're an 18 year old reading this who is unsure on which career path to choose, whether to be an entrepreneur or an employee; whether you are a middle aged man with a family & children; whether you are considering quitting your mundane day job or looking at creating a start-up company, if you can look at your life & place a specific monetary value on your time, it will undoubtedly help with your decision making & where you place your time & attention.

Naval's quote (above) was particularly addressing work & outsourcing tasks that were below your hourly wage, in order to free up more time in which you could allocate to working on your business. Whilst this is paramount for entrepreneurs & some high-flying employees alike, I would like to consider extrapolating that across other spheres of life.

For example, valuing your time at an hourly rate of say £100 (though Naval would say it should be much higher than that), would have a psychological impetus whereby you will be far less likely to waste time on tasks that are unfulfilling or that do not resonate with you at some deep level. It will allow you to better understand what it is that you value doing with your time & what it is that you don't find particularly fulfilling.

Many people go through life on autopilot. They never stop & take an audit of their actions & behaviours. Perhaps it's too painful to do so. Afterall, what have you achieved with your life?

Place a metaphorical price-tag on your time & watch the change. You do not have to share this with anyone, but it is a very handy cognitive process to undertake within your day-to-day activities. So, when it comes to the next time you have to travel to a random party, social engagement, or anything else that takes you away from your values & what's important to you, consider your hourly rate & whether or not your time could be better spent elsewhere.

As author Mark Manson says, "*...If it's not a "Fuck Yes;"* *then it's a "No.""* (114).

Value Hierarchies, Habits & Behaviour change

So how are we going to orchestrate our life, to take us from where we currently are, to where we want to be? What needs to change? Where should we start?

It is difficult to change your environment, especially if it is all you've ever known. Why else would so many people go through the struggle to get clean from drugs, alcohol, gambling & whole matter of other addictions only to fall back into the same routines when returning to their original environment?

If you are, roughly speaking, the average of the five people you are closest to, can you identify those people in your life? If there aren't five people, just focus on whoever you are closest to or who you pay the most attention to. I must make that caveat here as the increasingly pervasive loneliness that permeates our culture is undoubtedly leading some people to become more engaged with individuals online, as opposed to those in their immediate vicinity.

What values do these people hold?
How do they conduct themselves?
How do they live their lives?
If somebody were to tell you that you are like one of these people, would that be a compliment or an insult?

As we noted in the earlier chapter on masculinity; James Clear has a great passage in his book 'Atomic Habits' where he addresses this subject area. *"Surround yourself with people who have the habits you want to have yourself"* (32). He continues with the following addition, *"Join a culture where your desired behaviour is the normal behaviour"* (33). The author also states that, *"You don't have to be the victim of your environment. You can also be the architect of it"* (34).

Your environment can either drag you down into 'hell' or propel you up into 'heaven'. Try to understand these terms as metaphors for the worst outcome (hell) & the best outcome (heaven) – this will make more sense as you read on.

Hierarchy of values

"You have a hierarchy of values, you have to… otherwise you can't act, or you're painfully confused" (115).

In a society that has ascribed virtue to being busy, you may think that things aren't so bad because you're constantly in action. However, being busy can often just mean being chaotic & that is far from useful. Even if you dedicate yourself to achieving things & busying yourself with life, you will find yourself all over the place & lacking direction. As mentioned earlier, it doesn't matter how hard you work if you are going in the wrong direction. *"If a man knows not to which port he sails, no wind is favourable"* – Seneca.

By creating a hierarchy of values, you allow yourself the ability to co-ordinate your life around such a thing. In fact, Jordan Peterson has said in the past that whatever the highest value is in your life, it is that which *"serves the function of God for you"* (115). This use of religion as a metaphorical subtext to life, & in particular the concept of *'God'* in this respect, can generate a more profound understanding of how our values formulate around such a colossal entity, transcending the physical domain & revealing itself in our daily actions.

This may appear vague or contentious & I am very aware that it is a concept that may be met with a degree of resistance. This is perhaps due to the fact that our Western society is, in its current state, so secular. Nevertheless, you can interpret the above statement in the following way: What God is to Christians (& the same goes for all other major religions) is no different to the relationship you find yourself in when you enact yourself towards your highest value.

Under this premise, you can find some people today coming to the conclusion that nobody is actually an Atheist or secular in their beliefs. We all believe in something. However, in the absence of the church in modern times, people have found meaning through other avenues. Examples of this can stretch from supporting a sports team, a political party, a rock band or musician, a workplace, job or career, right the way through to simple hedonistic pleasure or the current socio-cultural issue that presents itself in the public consciousness.

"You have a hierarchy of values… whatever is at the top of that hierarchy of values serves the function of God for you" (115).

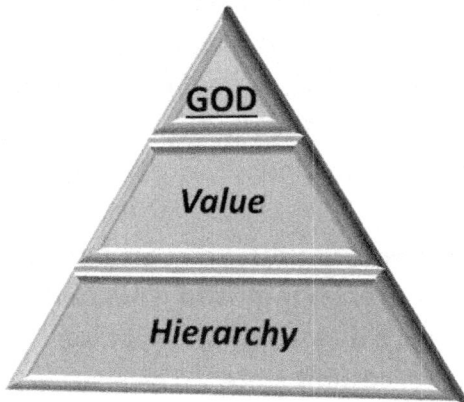

Having a goal is great. Something to work towards is fantastic… provided you are actually working towards it! This is because, at a neurochemical level, positive emotion (dopamine) is released in the *pursuit* of a goal. As we documented earlier in relation to dopamine, *"it's not the pursuit of happiness, but it's the happiness of the pursuit"* (30).

Outcome goals vs Process & Performance goals

Until recently, dopamine has generally been associated with the achievement of goals &, whilst this remains true, it is actually the process of moving forward (be that literally or figuratively) that elicits a profound response in positive emotion. So, as you move yourself towards such a goal you will likely obtain a healthy release of dopamine. The problem here is one that is often visible in our role models & in those who have achieved some 'celebrity status'... what happens once you have achieved your goals?

Whilst there may be substantial distance between where you are today & where you are striving to be, it is vitally important I cover the area here. If you are reading this book, if you are looking to make your life better & improve as a man, why would you not achieve the goals you have set out for your life?

These types of goals are known as 'outcome goals'. Outcome goals do not come without their own problems. They are explicitly binary. You either achieve your goal or you don't. This can be devastating if your entire life purpose was to achieve a particular goal, just to have nothing to follow it with.

Essentially, it is a zero-sum game. If you do not attain the specific goal, you have failed. Even if you do achieve the goal, you are faced with a further problem – this one perhaps even more destructive.

You have completed your life task... where do you go from here?

Professor Sapolsky's quote (above) becomes self-evident again here. If you aren't progressing toward something, it will be difficult to feel positive about what you are doing. In relation to the earlier chapter where we spoke about the 'Inner child' or our 'parts', we frequently observe our role models excelling at their chosen field & raising the bar in whatever industry they exist within. However, once they get to the top, or achieve what they set out to do, many end up turning to some kind of vice or coping mechanism that often ends up becoming self-destructive. Lost & bewildered (& now suffering at the hands of their own 'success'), they will turn to the world & ask; "*Wasn't this supposed to be the answer?*"

This occurs in every aspect of our lives. We may not realize it consciously, but we are all running off a script in our head where we want to achieve certain things, like tick-boxes for our lives. Perhaps these achievements resonate with us deeply, or perhaps they have been placed upon us through our culture & our early socialisation in our childhood. Either way, many of us will be at least partially aware of a point in the future where our tick-boxes will be complete.
Let's say you have the high paid job, you have the wife & the kids, you have the nice house & the fancy car. Only then will you come face to face with the most unsettling question of your life... *what now?*

It may be helpful at this point to revisit two earlier statements made in the book. Firstly, the striking example from Dr Jordan Peterson's book '12 Rules for Life'; "*One forty-something client told me his vision, formulated by his younger self: "I see myself retired, sitting on a tropical beach, drinking margaritas in the sunshine." That's not a plan. That's a travel poster. After eight margaritas, you're only fit to await the hangover. After three weeks of margarita-filled days, if you have any sense, you're bored stiff & self-disgusted. In a year, or less, you're pathetic.*" (24).

Furthermore, 'Rogan's Difficulty and Value Conflation';
"Look at the car he's driving, look at the watch he's wearing, look at the girl he's with. That's unattainable to many people, so it seems valuable. But when you attain it you realise that it's not valuable, it's just difficult to get" (102).
These things look like they have value, so most people spend their time & money pursuing them. Yet, in reality, they were actually just difficult to get.

So what is it you are aiming to accomplish?
Is that what you want for your life or is it actually just what you think you want?

Be very careful about having one sole outcome goal from which your happiness depends on. To take a recent, real-world example, the heavyweight boxer Tyson Fury literally fought his way to the top of the heavyweight division & completed his life dream when he beat Wladimir Klitschko in Germany back in 2015. Yet, following that victory, he spiralled into a deep depression & ended up vacating his titles, whilst entering a new fight – one with suicidal ideation. Fury has been very open with this ordeal &, whilst there may or may not have been underlying issues & other forces at play, it is fair to say that a large part of his particular struggle was a result of pedestalizing that one specific goal in his life… to be world champion.

I say this with a fair degree of certainty due to some interviews that surfaced around the time, documenting that period in Mr Fury's life, as well as the years that followed.

Firstly, he made an unprecedented return to boxing, dominating the entire heavyweight division. More importantly though were the changes he made regarding his reasons & motivations for continuing with his career. Yes, he had the desire to win titles & be the best heavyweight in the world, but at a more foundational level he knew that daily training & being in the gym was what he enjoyed & what kept him going.
Now his sole focus wasn't on the outcome, but rather on the process.

Incorporating 'process' goals & 'performance' goals alongside 'outcome' goals is a superior long-term strategy for success (116)(117). These types of goals, as you may imagine, are predicated on an assessment of how you are progressing toward an end goal. They require a degree of introspection & force you to be present, in the moment, reflecting on your habits & behaviours.
You can actually leverage dopamine in this way. By assessing what you are doing well, & by acknowledging your progress towards your goal, you will likely get a healthy release of dopamine throughout your journey. You can therefore experience little win after little win, over & over again. In doing so the journey quite literally becomes the destination. Bingo!

With a large amount of this book being directed towards setting goals & working towards your highest values, you could be easily forgiven for throwing your hands in the air in exasperation after comprehending the advantages of process & performance goals & the detriment of holding solely outcome goals.

What I am *not* saying here is to forget about your outcome goals altogether. The world is a competitive place & there is likely to be many people out there that have the same outcome goals as you. Success will not simply present itself at your door. To get to where you want to go you must first address your *'system'*. Again, we must look towards James Clear's book 'Atomic Habits' for inspiration, *"you do not rise to the level of your goals. You fall to the level of your systems"* (118).

Let's take an example; if two boxers are in a fight, they both have the goal to win… but someone's going to have to take a swing. Or, to take the example in the book, *"the goal in any team sport is to finish with the best score, but it would be ridiculous to spend the whole game staring at the scoreboard"* (119). Clear also includes a quote from three-time Super Bowl winner Bill Walsh that beautifully sums up the emphasis on improving your system; *"The score take's care of itself"* (120).

It isn't the goal itself that matters, it's what you do to get there. How are you playing the game? What actions & behaviours are present, & better yet consistent, in your daily life?

Having a goal does not make you successful. You have to execute on the actions, habits & behaviours that move you in that direction.

What are you doing today to get yourself one step closer to where you want to be?
I have a motto that I live by; *"1% better every single day"*.

Status games & success

Whilst society may reward you financially for being highly skilled in a specific area, *you* decide what success is for you. I would argue that financial success is a shallow goal if you have the resources to already be financially secure. We know that any money earned above the level of security & comfort does not necessarily yield more happiness (121). Some people will no doubt still chase more & more financial success for the sole purpose of having more... or of having *enough*. Financial success is just one of many status games played in our world & it is one that won't go away anytime soon.

Absent of money, other status games will manifest & perpetuate in their place. Whether that is the business game, the social media game, the fitness/aesthetics game, or some type of fame & attention (which you could argue incorporates all of the above), status games are not long-term games. They are simplistic at best & can be incredibly problematic when played for too long. They, like binary outcome goals, are zero-sum games.
Life is like an iterated trading game. As Naval Ravikant says, for success, *"play long-term games with long-term people. All returns in life, whether in wealth, relationships, or knowledge, come from compound interest"* (122).

Many individuals optimize for happiness in the moment, failing to understand that the height of any emotion never lasts long. They end up on the hedonic treadmill, searching for the next hit of dopamine. Regretfully, they will continue on that vicious cycle until the pain becomes too much to endure.

As the saying goes, *"you can lead a horse to water, but you cannot make it drink"*. People must actually want to change.

For many people, if they were to fall into a pot of money tomorrow, the likelihood that they would end up back in the same position that they started (or worse) down the line is, in my opinion, very likely. This, no doubt, would be amplified further if it involved betting/gambling.

Why do I say this?

Their achievement did not require an adequate, long-term strategy. Their financial success was predicated on pure luck, or on taking a (largely uncalculated) risk &, more than likely, being impulsive.

Some of the best indicators of long-term success is the ability to defer, or delay, gratification (123)(124) & to curb impulsivity (125).

There is certainly some merit to the statement *"discipline equals freedom"*.

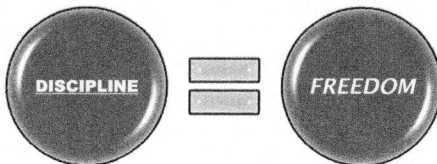

Creating the aforementioned value hierarchy allows you to identify what habits & behaviours fit into your system for success. It also shows you what habits & behaviours are detrimental to your success. We all have a different starting point here & that is okay. As the saying goes "*the best time to plant a tree was 20 years ago, the second best time is now*".
You cannot change the past, but the future is in your hands... it is directed by what you do in the present.

It is no small feat to change your behaviour, your identity, or your life. The neural wiring within you is already set in its place from years of repeated habits & actions, not to mention your internal beliefs & prior social conditioning. You will rub up against considerable resistance as you break down old (neural) connections & re-wire new ones, setting yourself up for long-term satisfaction & success. You must remember that it takes years & years of work to become an over-night success!

As we noted earlier, you will likely suffer from imposter syndrome... that is because you are changing, evolving & starting something new. This is unchartered territory. Do not fear it. Do not be deterred. Do the work.
"*A fit body, a calm mind, a house full of love. These things cannot be bought - they must be earned*" (126).

Thinking, planning & preparing can be great, but the only thing that will ease the mental burden of procrastination is to actually do the work. Getting yourself into action will alleviate the growing anxiety of inaction.

When planning for an activity or a goal, Ryan Holiday acknowledges, *"Talking and doing fight for the same resources"* (127).

Essentially, talking & planning can create an elevation in dopamine that would otherwise occur through doing the task at hand. This is all very well if you still do the task but will be detrimental for your progress if you do not.

"The more you're in, the more you win, & vice versa" – Jack Keyworth.

This cycles on repeat, stay in the game!
(And, yes, I did just quote myself again)

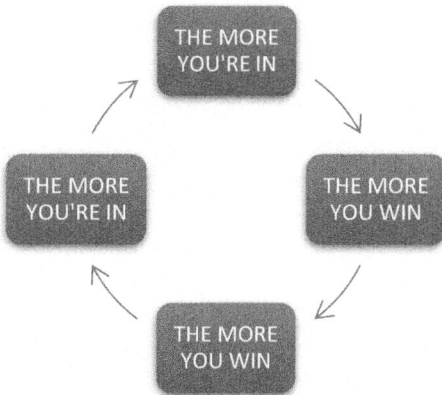

Doubt is removed by action.

"You don't become confident by shouting affirmations in the mirror, but by having a stack of undeniable proof that you are who you say you are. Outwork your self doubt" (128).

By taking a look over the horizon & toward your long-term success you will find that, through repetition, the friction between who you were & who you are will begin to disintegrate. This is a constant act of refinement. Nevertheless, you may be pleasantly surprised at just how far you can go based off consistent 1% improvements.

If you select your habits & behaviours carefully, shape your environment meticulously, & execute upon that which you say you will do, there really is no limit to what you can achieve!

Should you *not* do this, should you take the easy route of comfort & convenience that so many do, you may still succeed in fooling others, but you cannot fool yourself. That is, at least, not without harming your own integrity. *"You cannot cheat your way to success, even a cheetah gets caught eventually"* – Jack Keyworth. Yes, me again!

Distractions

How much time do you waste each day?
Think of the time you spend on social media, watching videos on YouTube, binging a TV series on Netflix, playing video games or smoking weed.
Like anything in life, there can be a time & place for many of the above activities (at least the legal ones anyway). There is no doubt that the TV series, the video games, the junk food, the sports game are all pleasurable experiences. That is exactly what they're designed to be.

Being flexible with your approach to life will always triumph over a rigid mindset – one in which you hold black & white rules around what is good & bad, what is acceptable & unacceptable. Nevertheless, as we recognized earlier, it is the ability to delay gratification that is one of the most crucial determinants of whether an individual ends up successful in their endeavours or not (123)(124).
The choices you make *will* influence the quality of your life, one way or another. The point I am attempting to make in this chapter is that our world currently has far more distractions in it than it has ever had before. Worse still, these distractions are becoming increasingly malevolent today because they are now generated by algorithms that are meticulously designed to keep you hooked on a particular website/channel/game/etc.

We are all at the mercy of these algorithms. Though they can sometimes appear beneficial in the moment, whether that be due to the ease of viewing, or for a unique browsing experience, or for a whole manner of other circumstances, these algorithms have the potential to culminate in a cascade of detrimental outcomes stretching across all facets of your life if not adequately managed.

Why do I refer to these activities as distractions?
I feel that anything placing 'you' as the product is undoubtedly a distraction due to its intention. If the goal is to hijack your attention & to hold your conscious awareness hostage (even if it appears to have been done willingly), I consider that to be a distraction. Through this process, your focus of attention has been taken away from something else.
I have no doubt that there are more important areas of your life in which you could place this time & attention. You are up against insurmountable odds, make no mistake about that. Nevertheless, in a society that is becoming ever more 'limbically hijacked', try to bring yourself into the present.

Ponder the following questions before moving on:
How much time are you spending outdoors?
How much time do you spend exercising?
How much time are you spending with friends & family?
How much of your life are you spending doing the things that truly matter?

As stated earlier in the book, you discriminate with every decision you make. If you prioritize the TV & video games more than being physically active & staying in shape that is your decision, but keep in mind your value hierarchy & whether you are acting in alignment with such values.
If, at this point, you look at your present life & feel truly content – in whatever manner that may be – that is also absolutely fine. You will not hear me saying you *have* to change. So long as you are not deceiving yourself, you do you!

On the other hand, if your life is not how you want it, if you could be more than you currently are (& you aspire to maximise your potential) you will need to remain disciplined & forthright in your day-to-day behaviours. This means you will need to do what is required first, before indulging in the pleasures of life that we are so fortunate to have today. You must become mindful of how it is you are operating & what it is you are prioritizing.
Are your actions conducive to your desired outcomes? Remember, *where attention goes, energy flows.*

Before the digital age, individuals found themselves more engaged with those around them – their family, their friends & their community. The magnanimous change within the last generation or two cannot be understated. Despite the world being more connected than ever, thanks to the internet &, branching off from that, social media, we find ourselves in a strange state of psychological diaspora. We are social animals. We crave social connection. Yet we continuously find ourselves on our phones & other devices today, oblivious to the physical world around us.

I'll refer again here to the work of Bruce K Alexander in the 1970's... that's right, we're talking about 'Rat Park'. These studies saw rats given water laced with drugs such as cocaine or heroin, stimulating the rats' pleasure response. The results showed that the rats would continuously press a lever to deliver the drug whilst avoiding all else – some of them all the way to death. However, when the rats were placed in a more natural environment, when they had gratifying social relationships & were able to play & have sex, few touched the drug filled water & none abused it to the point of death.
So, my question to you is this: Do you recognize this in your own life (drugs being considered a metaphor, of course)?

Rat Park carries with it such importance when looking at the state of our society today. Our globalized & digitally connected world can feel completely overwhelming. Equally, you can look at our evolution & see an enormous asymmetry to how we live today. Society is fragmented, we don't know our neighbours like we used to, for many of us our family may live on the other side of the country (or for some of us, the world) & many of us do not have an intimate partner (129) or any close friends at all (89). Whilst we are undoubtedly more connected than ever before, we are lacking sufficient depth in our relationships & are today becoming deficient in the real-world relationships that we depend upon as a species.

Once again, I will re-iterate the damning statement on Dr Alexander's website, under a segment titled 'Addiction: The View from Rat Park (2010)'.
"*I encounter human beings who really do not have a viable social or cultural life. They use their addictions as a way of coping with their dislocation*" (91).
The most damning statement is that which follows; "*the drug only becomes irresistible when the opportunity for normal social existence is destroyed*" (91).

The reason I have included Dr Alexander's work again here is because, whilst we know the statistics on loneliness & suicide (documented in the chapter titled 'Connection'), the compensatory mechanism for these issues can often take the form of compulsive behaviours, distracting us from our 'dislocation'. This can take many different forms; social media scrolling, gambling, bingeing TV, binge eating, alcohol consumption/binge drinking, abusing drugs, & even cutting, to name just a few.

Some of the above behaviours can, in fact, be considered 'self-harm'.
If any of these are true for you, please speak to a medical/healthcare professional, seek the appropriate help that's available to you, & speak to your friends & family. Do not be ashamed to do so. Help is available &, though it may not seem like it, there is a way through what you are currently feeling.

Below are some resources & contacts for your convenience, should you wish to use them (some numbers may incur a call charge):

- Call 999 if you are in a crisis
- Samaritans – call 116123 / email jo@samaritans.org
- MIND – call 03001233393
- Addaction – call 02072515860 / email info@addaction.org.uk
- Alcoholics Anonymous – call 08009177650 / email help@alcoholics-anonymous.org.uk
- Drink aware – call 02077669900 / email contact@drinkaware.co.uk
- DrugScience – www.drugscience.org.uk
- Anxiety UK – call 08444775774 / email support@anxietyuk.org.uk
- BEAT – call 03456341414 / email help@b-eat.co.uk

We often patch over our uncomfortable feelings with a consumer culture that wants both your attention & your money. We are all too happy to oblige. We want to be soothed & we want to have our fantasies stimulated... we want to be given a release from the stresses & mundanity of life.

As such, we binge TV shows, consume copious amounts of food & alcohol, & barely lift our heads out of our phones, not wanting to miss the latest craze or new headline story. Though these are all detrimental habits if disproportionately consumed, one of the most pertinent issues for men of this generation is pornography use.

Pornography

Not so long ago, if you wanted to see a naked woman you would have to buy a magazine from the top shelf of a local corner shop. That would be an awkward encounter at the checkout! (This was also a time when you paid with cash & there was an employee there to take your money & give you any change you were due.)
A few generations prior & the mere thought of a woman being underdressed would be enough to hijack a gentleman's attention. However, just like the movement from cash to cashless, & human to machine, the adult industry exploded with the onset of the digital age – particularly upon the transition to smart phones & the instant, unlimited access to adult websites they brought with them.

This specific distraction is of a monumental magnitude. You have naked women online at the click of a finger. No need to walk to the shop, no need to use your imagination. In relation to porn, men (& women) today have more access to explicit material & nudity than even the richest, most powerful King could have dreamt of in the past. Not only is this a huge distraction, it can be incredibly damaging over the long term.
This can be for a variety of reasons, ranging from difficulty in establishing & maintaining relationships (& possessing unrealistic expectations of such relationships), right the way through to all-out addiction.

It doesn't stop at porn though. This internet age has witnessed a bombardment of women (though it should be stated that some men also follow this path) either posting their bodies online in return for money (websites such as OnlyFans) or, perhaps more degradingly, posting half naked photos (& that is putting it generously) of themselves on their social media profiles in the hope of people 'liking' their photo.

Be mindful of how you curate your feed online & particularly on social media, it *will* influence your life.

It's an uphill battle for men to articulate themselves towards their highest values & away from vice due to their biological predisposition; "*after puberty men produce 20 times more testosterone than women, resulting in circulating testosterone concentrations 15-fold higher than in children or women of any age*" (130). Watching an attractive woman having crazy, acrobatic sex can be too much to resist. This is what is at our fingertips every single day.

It takes willpower not to think of sex as a man, let alone knowing you have an endless stream of attractive young women performing an unlimited array of sexual acts just a few clicks away on your phone.

Perhaps you aren't getting any sex in your life. Perhaps you are void of an intimate relationship. Maybe you are a virgin. As the world moves further into a digital era & social connections become less & less physical, you can begin to see how this could explode into a huge mess down the line (*pun intended*).

Could you make the argument that your work, your passion or your continuous path to self-improvement is just one big distraction?

You could do...

Under such a premise, the very act of reading itself could be considered an escape or a distraction from life.

Though this doesn't have to be the case.

I would argue here that, if reading this book & using it to improve your life is having the desired effect (self-improvement, a better quality of life, a route forward etc) then, distraction or not, you are receiving some benefit. Nevertheless, change is preceded by action. Application is key.

If, however, this book has been used as a distraction, to avoid 'doing' life & instead to retreat from the world, there may be something lying deeper within you that needs to be addressed.

Every individual reading this will be at a different point in their lives, having had different life experiences, & with different interpretations of those experiences.

The root cause isn't always going to be self-evident. Think of the iceberg analogy. What is it that's going on beneath the surface?

Let us reflect here on a fascinating insight we uncovered earlier from the late psychologist Carl Jung; *"no tree, it is said, can reach to heaven unless its roots reach down to hell"* (53).

Optimisation

I have not written this book to 'fix' or to counsel you.
That is not my intention, nor is it my area of expertise. In
fact, I would argue even so far as there is nothing to 'fix'.
There is no problem. What each of us have is our current
level of perception. Ultimately, you & I had no control
over our early conditioning, but this process of
maturation was unique in forming who we are today. Can
you reflect back on this without judgement & with full
acceptance?

Circumstance is objective. It is neutral. It is only when
met with a perception, an expectation, a subjective
interpretation, that there becomes a 'problem'.
Could it be your relationship to circumstance itself that is
causing you to suffer?

At this stage it is my hope that you have a better
understanding of yourself & what it is that constitutes
'you'. Now would be a great time to stop & to take a look
back at various sections in the book. What areas do you
feel are important for you right now, at this stage of your
life? Perhaps you have gone through an unsettling event,
a job loss, a break up, an injury or some other change in
circumstance.
Re-familiarise yourself with the particular areas you find
most applicable to where you currently are. Reflect on
your boundaries, reflect on your value hierarchy, identify
with where you are & where you are heading.

Is your environment conducive to your goals & aspirations?

You may recall earlier the acknowledgment of an individuals' intrinsic motivation coming from one of two different areas. In the pursuit of a goal or an aim, one will either be fuelled by running *toward* something or by running *away* from something else – with much potential for overlap.
Generally, you are either motivated by moving *'to'* something or *'away'* from something else. Some 'successful' entrepreneurs will openly state that it is the latter which has yielded their success.

Driving away from something will likely generate a greater magnitude of response than working toward something. Use this fuel at your own peril.
Tapping into pain & suffering for motivation can be an effective tool but be mindful of the fact that it is a 'tool' & should not be running (or more-so *ruining*) your life.
Pain is one hell of a motivator & many people would testify that a behaviour is only changed when the pain of staying the same becomes worse than the pain of change. If the pain is not bad enough it is likely that, for most people, the change will not occur. Despite that, avoiding what needs to be done can only last so long. Eventually you will face the music, one way or another.
You can suffer now or be forced to suffer later.

In a podcast with Joe Rogan, Chris Williamson uncovers how this obstacle can prevent forward motion in life, uncovering the concept of 'The Region Beta Paradox', quoted below.

"Imagine that if you were to go a mile or less you would walk it & if you were to go more than a mile you would drive it. Paradoxically, you would go two miles quicker than you would go one mile. So that means that sometimes worse situations can be better than better situations, & this is an issue when, if you only decide to act after you cross a certain threshold of 'badness' or whatever, you can end up being stuck in region beta...

So for instance, the friend that should leave his job, really really needs to leave his job, but it's just about passable... his boss isn't that much of a d*ck, maybe the benefits are okay... whatever. Or the person that's in a relationship with someone that they really don't want to stay with & it's not that brilliant, but it's not that bad, they don't abuse them... everything's okay. The person who stays in an apartment that's got some mould on the ceiling, but it's not too much mould, & whatever...

All of these people would be better off if their situations were worse because it would galvanise them into actually doing something... You can get stuck in this chasm of comfortable complacency that sits somewhere in the middle.

If things are good... great, no problem. If things are bad... great, activation energy to go & make them good. If things are just about passable, you end up being comfortably numb" (131).

Who am I to say what or how you should fuel your desire? Whatever keeps you in the game longer sounds like a great plan to me. No matter what you accomplish, no matter the magnitude of your achievements in this world, it is likely that no one will remember you in three generations time. That may seem nihilistic, yet it is in fact anything but.

If you are doing what you are doing under the pretence of receiving recognition or of serving your ego (which is quite likely) it will probably not be something that truly speaks to your soul, nor is it something that will move the world forward. Remember my 'ABC mental model' we addressed earlier; act benevolently, for the highest good – be that for both yourself & for the world.

Our habits & behaviours can be made easier or harder (& therefore less likely to be adhered to) depending upon how we shape our environment.

As we have noted several times now, an environment that is conducive to your goals &/or the life you wish to lead will give you an excellent chance of success.

However, an environment that runs contradictory to that of your idealized life will cause constant friction & resistance.

Admittedly, we have addressed this in the earlier chapters so I'm aware that this may seem like I'm teaching you to suck eggs, but lock in because we are about to go as simplistic as we can here... *neurons that fire together, wire together*.

If you repeat an action enough times, it <u>will</u> become ingrained.

Let's say you are struggling to stay off of social media or you are trying to stop watching porn. Try deleting the apps or start logging out each time you do use them. This creates a barrier between what is likely to be an automated & almost unconscious process.

In order to enact a change in habitual behaviour there needs to be some friction, or at least some space, between the thought & the action. Remember, here, the famous quote attributed to Victor Frankl; *"Between stimulus & response there is a space. In that space is our power to choose our response"*.

You could make it that you can only do the behaviour whilst going out for a walk or whilst doing a workout (though that may be quite difficult with the porn use). Better still, see if you can meet that underlying psychological need by completely swapping out the current behaviour for one that is more beneficial for your health or more aligned to your goal/s. Perhaps the porn use or chronic social media scrolling is the result of a lack of social connection in the physical world – as we alluded to earlier in the book.

Could it be more advantageous to enrol in a new hobby, join a sports team or meet with friends?

Depending on your value hierarchy (of which you hopefully have a reasonable idea of now) you will be able to identify what habits are beneficial for you & what habits will be detrimental.

Incorporate 'good' habits over time. Make them small & easy to integrate, then slowly build upon them.

On the other hand, generate resistance between you & your 'bad' habits, those that are leading you away from your desired outcome/s.

Keep stacking evidence that you are the person you claim to be by continuously improving your life 1% at a time.

<u>We are what we repeatedly do.</u>

So, I'll ask you once again... Who are *<u>YOU</u>*?

Conclusion

So here we are at the end of the book...
It has been a great pleasure to share with you my knowledge & to be able to compile it into this book for you. It is my hope that you have taken the information on board & are able to use it to improve the quality of your life.
This book has hopefully provided you with the foundations from which to propel yourself forwards in your life &, through the utilization of the different concepts, practices & insights, the ability to maximise your potential.

By assessing where you are & where you want to go, & by adopting maximal responsibility for your life, you are now ready to take on the world.
This is just the beginning of your journey & I am proud to have shared it with you through this book.
The work doesn't end here... just as we spoke of in earlier chapters, the aim is not to complete the game, rather it is to enjoy the ride. Continue to improve yourself & continue to improve your life, one step at a time.

Show patience, both in yourself & in your progress forward.
In doing so, you should, however, be mindful to never become too absorbed in your goals, such that you fail to attain a level of harmony with life.
And yet, we all need a purpose.

Each of us must fork out a path from which we are to continue onwards.

As stated earlier in the book; Don't aim for happiness. Aim for purpose & meaning... take absolute accountability for your life.

Or, as Friedrich Nietzsche expertly remarked, *"He whose life has a why can bear almost any how"* (14).

Only you can change yourself &, if you can do that, you truly can change the world!

JACK KEYWORTH

Now that you have a completed this book, why not consider purchasing my health & wellbeing book: "SENSE Great Health"?

Spanning the most important factors that influence health-span (some of which we have covered here) as well as insights into how to train for different goals & live the most purposeful & productive life possible, there is a wealth of information to be had here!

I have no doubt that you will find benefit from SENSE Great Health, just as I hope you have from Men's Optimisation Bible.

So, what are you waiting for?

References:

(1) 'The Almanack of Naval Ravikant' by Eric Jorgenson, page 33.

(2) Howes R.J. and T.G. Carskadon. "Test-Retest Reliabilities of the Myers-Briggs Type Indicator as a function of Mood Changes." Research in Psychological Type, Vol. 2, No. 1 (1979), pp. 67-72.

(3) McCarley, N., and T.G. Carskadon 1983 Test-retest reliabilities of scales and subscales of the Myers-Briggs Type Indicator and of criteria for clinical interpretive hypotheses involving them. Research in Psychological Type6:24-36.

(4) Daniel Druckman, Robert A. Bjork. Commission on Behavioural and Social Sciences and Education. National Research Council, National Academy Press. Effectiveness of Applications, page 100.
https://nap.nationalacademies.org/read/1580/chapter/8#100

(5) What is Self Authoring? https://www.selfauthoring.com

(6) Jordan B Peterson, 18th April 2017. 2017 Personality 18: Biology & Traits: Openness/Intelligence/Creativity I (youtube.com). YouTube.

(7) Higgins DM, Peterson JB, Pihl RO, Lee AGM. Prefrontal cognitive ability, intelligence, Big Five personality, and the prediction of advanced academic and workplace performance. J Pers Soc Psychol. 2007 Aug;93(2):298-319. doi: 10.1037/0022-3514.93.2.298. PMID: 17645401.

(8) Jimmy Carr, Before & Laughter page 24.

(9) Modern Wisdom podcast, 9th October 2023. Podcast episode #691, Jimmy Carr – The Secret Hacks For Living A Fulfilled Life. https://open.spotify.com/episode/1LjGF1dmYWnPhIkDLUvATC Spotify.

(10) Cohen S, Doyle WJ, Skoner DP, Rabin BS, Gwaltney JM Jr. Social ties and susceptibility to the common cold. JAMA. 1997 Jun 25;277(24):1940-4. PMID: 9200634

(11) Umberson D, Crosnoe R, Reczek C. Social Relationships and Health Behavior Across Life Course. Annu Rev Sociol. 2010 Aug

1;36:139-157. doi: 10.1146/annurev-soc-070308-120011. PMID: 21921974; PMCID: PMC3171805

(12) Tiwari SC. Loneliness: A disease? Indian J Psychiatry. 2013 Oct;55(4):320-2. doi: 10.4103/0019-5545.120536. PMID: 24459300; PMCID: PMC3890922

(13) @AlexHormozi, 30th August 2023. https://x.com/AlexHormozi/status/1696844003289804827 X.

(14) Nietzsche, F.W. & Kaufmann, W.A. (1982). The portable Nietzsche. New York: Penguin Classics (Maxims and Arrows 12).

(15) Jordan Peterson, 12 rules for life, rule 7, page 161.

(16) Jordan Peterson, 12 rules for life, page 172.

(17) Sally Weale, 12th May 2016. 'UK's university gender gap is a national scandal, says thinktank'. The Guardian. https://www.theguardian.com/education/2016/may/12/university-gender-gap-scandal-thinktank-men

(18) Philip Zimbardo, Nikita Coulombe. 14th January 2021. 'Young Men and Society: We Will Only Get Out What We Put In'. Institute for Family Studies. https://ifstudies.org/blog/young-men-and-society-we-will-only-get-out-what-we-put-in

(19) Modern Wisdom podcast, 23rd October 2023. Podcast episode #697, Konstantin Kisin – Why Does It Feel Like Everyone Is Losing Their Minds? https://open.spotify.com/episode/2cNqg2lJdvOlvV6wNkuKWx Spotify.

(20) Sagar-Ouriaghli I, Godfrey E, Bridge L, Meade L, Brown JSL. Improving Mental Health Service Utilization Among Men: A Systematic Review and Synthesis of Behavior Change Techniques Within Interventions Targeting Help-Seeking. Am J Mens Health. 2019 May-Jun;13(3):1557988319857009. doi: 10.1177/1557988319857009. PMID: 31184251; PMCID: PMC6560805.

(21) The Jordan B Peterson Podcast, 17th November 2019. 'Being a victim'. https://open.spotify.com/episode/0kjoVkGDzx6u22qd4OtTbc Spotify.

(22) Jordan Peterson, 12 rules for life, page 161.

(23) The Jordan B. Peterson Podcast, 23rd May 2017. 'Introduction to the Idea of God'.
https://open.spotify.com/episode/3eP9ZWnpkiJIBpxy3alTu9
Spotify.

(24) Jordan Peterson, 12 Rules for Life, page 210/211.

(25) The Joe Rogan Experience, 28th November 2016. Podcast episode #877 - Jordan Peterson.
https://open.spotify.com/episode/4Ks3GyUM8Zsy5Ax5fnm7ev
Spotify.

(26) Jocko Podcast, 7th February 2018. Podcast episode #112 – Jordan Peterson.
https://open.spotify.com/episode/75vL2ZbwkUjvWiRvqSglUq
Spotify.

(27) Adapted from comedian Chris Rock's infamous stand-up comedy clip; "*only women, children, & dogs are loved unconditionally... a man is only loved under the condition that he provides something*".

(28) Infinite Loops podcast 28th December 2023. Podcast episode #195, George Mack – The Game of Life.
https://open.spotify.com/episode/73khk4NG4Ap495xfoTJZMr?si=3V1qSvGURTK4ui784ocKnw&nd=1&dlsi=97c481f3d7014578
Spotify.

(29) Written by Hope Cristol, reviewed by Smitha Bhandari, MD. 19th July 2023. 'What is Dopamine?' WebMD.
https://www.webmd.com/mental-health/what-is-dopamine

(30) Modern Wisdom podcast 14th October 2023. Podcast episode #693, Dr Robert Sapolsky – The Shocking New Science Of How To Manage Your Stress.
https://open.spotify.com/episode/7l0bj3agmdH5kaSiyi9UJu
Spotify.

(31) The Weekend University, 25th August 2023. Dr Anna Lembke – 'Resetting Your Brain's Dopamine Balance'
https://www.youtube.com/watch?v=Lslae8UeWGE – YouTube.

(32) James Clear, Atomic Habits page 117.

(33)James Clear, Atomic Habits page 117.

(34)James Clear, Atomic Habits page 84.

(35)@ChrisWillx, 15th August 2021.

https://www.instagram.com/chriswillx/p/CSl7RveoXFP/
Instagram.

(36)The Joe Rogan Experience, 29th May 2012. Podcast episode #222.

https://open.spotify.com/episode/13vqfFl7bslreyQ0BA3CE4
Spotify.

(37)Jordan Peterson, 12 Rules for Life, rule 4 page 85.

(38)Adapted from multiple interviews/lectures from renowned psychologist & author, Dr Jordan Peterson.

(39)Modern Wisdom podcast 16th January 2023. Podcast episode #577, David Goggins – This Is How To Master Your Life.

https://open.spotify.com/episode/328DFHU0KBOzgQKfz2Fahb
Spotify.

(40)Modern Wisdom podcast 21st July 2022. Podcast episode #502, Jocko Willink – Creating An Unbreakable Mindset.

https://open.spotify.com/episode/3C8FfEk8gPfp1gO6SaEYRi
Spotify.

(41) Modern Wisdom podcast, 17th February 2022. Podcast episode #436, Dr Jordan Peterson – Your Life Is Built For More.

https://open.spotify.com/episode/1qWOQzfLBSYmCFK95yEzcL
Spotify.

(42)Know Thyself podcast, 3rd December 2023. Podcast episode #66, Peter Crone – Transcend Self-Made Suffering & Discover Your Inherent Worth.

https://open.spotify.com/episode/305uxJlGjjj1hFStd0uq1F
Spotify.

(43)Jordan Peterson, 12 rules for life, page 43.

(44)   Raul Lopez Jr, 29th March 2017. 'Heal the Boy and the Man will Appear'. Tony Robbins.

https://www.youtube.com/watch?v=vjwf9IlxUNY – YouTube.

(45)@bc_serna, 1st August 2023.

https://www.instagram.com/reel/CvYeFTnreLx/ Instagram.

(46) Hill, Andrew & Witcher, Chad & Gotwals, John & Leyland, Anna. (2015). A Qualitative Study of Perfectionism Among Self-Identified Perfectionists in Sport and the Performing Arts. Sport, Exercise, and Performance Psychology. 4. 10.1037/spy0000041.

(47) The Joe Rogan Experience, 2nd August 2022. Podcast episode #1851 – Chris Williamson. https://open.spotify.com/episode/3XMmLbHR7MUJsvrs3pmDWx Spotify.

(48) NHS, The Stress Bucket – A model for understanding stress. https://www.hey.nhs.uk/wp/wp-content/uploads/2020/08/OHC_StressBucket.pdf

(49) Edwards, Eleanor & Interthal, Heidrun & Mcqueen, Heather. (2021). Managing your mind: how simple activities within the curriculum can improve undergraduate students' mental health and wellbeing. New Directions in the Teaching of Physical Sciences. 10.29311/ndtps.v0i16.3588. (Adapted from Williams & Powell, 2017).

(50) The Huberman Lab podcast, 20th February 2023. How to Breathe Correctly for Optimal Health, Mood, Learning & Performance. https://open.spotify.com/episode/0mPoOepkOJZlnPMNvPC10h Spotify.

(51) @hubermanlab, 22nd February 2023. https://www.instagram.com/reel/Co-rZhisw0m/ Instagram.

(52) Modern Wisdom, 1st June 2020. Podcast episode #178, George Mack – Mental Models 103. https://open.spotify.com/episode/1uByOiftvhdvDkgoNtnNYs Spotify.

(53) Collected works of C. G. Jung, Volume 9 (part 2) Aion: Researchers into the Phenomenology of the Self.

(54) Naska A, Oikonomou E, Trichopoulou A, Psaltopoulou T, Trichopoulos D. Siesta in healthy adults and coronary mortality in the general population. Arch Intern Med. 2007 Feb

12;167(3):296-301. doi: 10.1001/archinte.167.3.296. PMID: 17296887.

(55) Pandi-Perumal SR, Spence DW, Srivastava N, Kanchibhotla D, Kumar K, Sharma GS, Gupta R, Batmanabane G. The Origin and Clinical Relevance of Yoga Nidra. Sleep Vigil. 2022;6(1):61-84. doi: 10.1007/s41782-022-00202-7. Epub 2022 Apr 23. PMID: 35496325; PMCID: PMC9033521.

(56) Netz Y. Is the Comparison between Exercise and Pharmacologic Treatment of Depression in the Clinical Practice Guideline of the American College of Physicians Evidence-Based? Front Pharmacol. 2017 May 15;8:257. doi: 10.3389/fphar.2017.00257. PMID: 28555108; PMCID: PMC5430071.

(57) CDC, Physical Activity Basics. 20th December 2023. Physical Activity for Adults: An Overview. Physical Activity for Adults: An Overview | Physical Activity Basics | CDC

(58) NHS, last reviewed 4th August 2021. Physical activity guidelines for adults aged 19 to 64. https://www.nhs.uk/live-well/exercise/exercise-guidelines/physical-activity-guidelines-for-adults-aged-19-to-64/#:~:text=do%20at%20least%20150%20minutes,a%20week%2C%20or%20every%20day

(59) Modern Wisdom, 10th April 2023. Podcast episode #613 – Dr Peter Attia. https://open.spotify.com/episode/69hQNXZw4s5gFA871GWjy0 Spotify.

(60) Modern Wisdom, 9th October 2023. Podcast episode #691, Jimmy Carr – The Secret Hacks For Living A Fulfilled Life. https://open.spotify.com/episode/1LjGF1dmYWnPhlkDLUvATC Spotify / @ChrisWillx, 13th October 2023. https://www.instagram.com/p/CyWE4y1oPC3/?img_index=6 Instagram.

(61) James Clear, Atomic Habits page 104.

(62) The Joe Rogan Experience, 26th July 2017. Podcast episode #989 – Dorian Yates.

https://open.spotify.com/episode/37oiQgSHlql6cJp6l93Te0
Spotify.

(63) Yamashita Y. The 3-Minute Burpee Test: A Minimalistic Alternative to the Conventional Estimated Oxygen Uptake Test. Cureus. 2023 Mar 6;15(3):e35841. doi: 10.7759/cureus.35841. PMID: 37033564; PMCID: PMC10080365.

(64) Foster C, Farland CV, Guidotti F, Harbin M, Roberts B, Schuette J, Tuuri A, Doberstein ST, Porcari JP. The Effects of High Intensity Interval Training vs Steady State Training on Aerobic and Anaerobic Capacity. J Sports Sci Med. 2015 Nov 24;14(4):747-55. PMID: 26664271; PMCID: PMC4657417.

(65) Kim Y, White T, Wijndaele K, Westgate K, Sharp SJ, Helge JW, Wareham NJ, Brage S. The combination of cardiorespiratory fitness and muscle strength, and mortality risk. Eur J Epidemiol. 2018 Oct;33(10):953-964. doi: 10.1007/s10654-018-0384-x. Epub 2018 Mar 28. PMID: 29594847; PMCID: PMC6153509.

(66) Bohannon RW. Grip Strength: An Indispensable Biomarker For Older Adults. Clin Interv Aging. 2019 Oct 1;14:1681-1691. doi: 10.2147/CIA.S194543. PMID: 31631989; PMCID: PMC6778477.

(67) James Clear, Atomic Habits page 38.

(68) How Long Can You Go Without Sleep? Anne Marie Conlon, New Scientist. https://www.newscientist.com/question/how-long-can-you-go-without-sleep/

(69) NLBI – How Sleep Works. Last updated 24th March 2022. How much sleep is enough? https://www.nhibi.nih.gov/health/sleep/how-much-sleep

(70) Cohen S, Doyle WJ, Alper CM, Janicki-Deverts D, Turner RB. Sleep habits and susceptibility to the common cold. Arch Intern Med. 2009 Jan 12;169(1):62-7. doi: 10.1001/archinternmed.2008.505. PMID: 19139325; PMCID: PMC2629403.

(71) Watson A, Johnson M, Sanfilippo J. Decreased Sleep Is an Independent Predictor of In-Season Injury in Male Collegiate Basketball Players. Orthop J Sports Med. 2020 Nov

9;8(11):2325967120964481. doi: 10.1177/2325967120964481. PMID: 33225012; PMCID: PMC7658528.

(72) Erren TC, Falaturi P, Morfeld P, Knauth P, Reiter RJ, Piekarski C. Shift work and cancer: the evidence and the challenge. Dtsch Arztebl Int. 2010 Sep;107(38):657-62. doi: 10.3238/arztebl.2010.0657. Epub 2010 Sep 24. PMID: 20953253; PMCID: PMC2954516.

(73) Gan Y, Yang C, Tong X, Sun H, Cong Y, Yin X, Li L, Cao S, Dong X, Gong Y, Shi O, Deng J, Bi H, Lu Z. Shift work and diabetes mellitus: a meta-analysis of observational studies. Occup Environ Med. 2015 Jan;72(1):72-8. doi: 10.1136/oemed-2014-102150. Epub 2014 Jul 16. PMID: 25030030.

(74) Karlsson B, Alfredsson L, Knutsson A, Andersson E, Torén K. Total mortality and causespecific mortality of Swedish shift- and dayworkers in the pulp and paper industry in 1952-2001. Scand J Work Environ Health. 2005 Feb;31(1):30-5. doi: 10.5271/sjweh.845. PMID: 15751616.

(75) @hubermanlab, 7th December 2022. https://www.instagram.com/reel/Cl31uJbJQEa/ Instagram.

(76) Sagawa Y, Kondo H, Matsubuchi N, Takemura T, Kanayama H, Kaneko Y, Kanbayashi T, Hishikawa Y, Shimizu T. Alcohol has a dose-related effect on parasympathetic nerve activity during sleep. Alcohol Clin Exp Res. 2011 Nov;35(11):2093-100. doi: 10.1111/j.1530-0277.2011.01558.x. Epub 2011 Aug 16. PMID: 21848959.

(77) Park SY, Oh MK, Lee BS, Kim HG, Lee WJ, Lee JH, Lim JT, Kim JY. The Effects of Alcohol on Quality of Sleep. Korean J Fam Med. 2015 Nov;36(6):294-9. doi: 10.4082/kjfm.2015.36.6.294. Epub 2015 Nov 20. PMID: 26634095; PMCID: PMC4666864.

(78) Simou E, Britton J, Leonardi-Bee J. Alcohol and the risk of sleep apnoea: a systematic review and meta-analysis. Sleep Med. 2018 Feb;42:38-46. doi: 10.1016/j.sleep.2017.12.005. Epub 2018 Jan 3. PMID: 29458744; PMCID: PMC5840512.

(79) Josie Clarke, 1st February 2023. 'Huge' differences in high street coffee caffeine amounts, study finds. The Standard.

https://www.standard.co.uk/news/uk/coffee-caffeine-amounts-uk-pret-costa-starbucks-greggs-b1057032.html

(80) Institute of Medicine (US) Committee on Military Nutrition Research. Caffeine for the Sustainment of Mental Task Performance: Formulations for Military Operations. Washington (DC): National Academies Press (US); 2001. 2, Pharmacology of Caffeine, page 25. Available from: https://www.ncbi.nlm.nih.gov/books/NBK223808/

(81) Guest NS, VanDusseldorp TA, Nelson MT, Grgic J, Schoenfeld BJ, Jenkins NDM, Arent SM, Antonio J, Stout JR, Trexler ET, Smith-Ryan AE, Goldstein ER, Kalman DS, Campbell BI. International society of sports nutrition position stand: caffeine and exercise performance. J Int Soc Sports Nutr. 2021 Jan 2;18(1):1. doi: 10.1186/s12970-020-00383-4. PMID: 33388079; PMCID: PMC7777221.

(82) Spiegel K, Tasali E, Penev P, Van Cauter E. Brief communication: Sleep curtailment in healthy young men is associated with decreased leptin levels, elevated ghrelin levels, and increased hunger and appetite. Ann Intern Med. 2004 Dec 7;141(11):846-50. doi: 10.7326/0003-4819-141-11-200412070-00008. PMID: 15583226.

(83) Matthew Walker, Why We Sleep, page 42.

(84) Matthew Walker, Why We Sleep, page 47.

(85) Ten Percent Happier with Dan Harris, 31st October 2022. Podcast episode 'The science of making and keeping friends' – Robin Dunbar. https://open.spotify.com/episode/3PToUZGYCY7cKgMIFJqzMh Spotify.

(86) Vishesh Raisinghani, 24th July 2023. 'Just 71% of young males held a full-time job in 2021 — that's a big drop from 85% in 1980. Here's why millions of men are dropping out of the workforce at an alarming rate'. Yahoo! finance. https://finance.yahoo.com/news/just-71-young-males-2021-180000984.html?guccounter=1&guce_referrer=aHR0cHM6Ly93d3cuZ29vZ2xlLmNvLnVrLw&guce_referrer_sig=AQAAAAmsJoitr

MAK4E3Qv_x8sRPbUPa8L21v3kJ_vRXZqmEg4VIERF0TgCWbHvr
TSPAqDVCKeG1oR9kejxfuqZBEmgAHsypEir28dwuEWVEF6iNY1h
yb6c5IPEH07Zlu9_6VHVPuCgUXOKLI8e90OTYl7QZ7V3YIH360
m7XMYOoNe9I0

(87) Jonathan Rothwell, 17th January 2023. 'Scarred Boys, Idle Men;
Family Adversity, Poor Health, and Male Labor Force
Participation'. Institute for Family Studies.
https://ifstudies.org/blog/scarred-boys-idle-men-family-
adversity-poor-health-and-male-labor-force-participation

(88) ONS Census 2021. 14th May 2024. Male employment rate
(aged16-64, seasonally adjusted): %.
https://www.ons.gov.uk/employmentandlabourmarket/peoplei
nwork/employmentandemployeetypes/timeseries/mgsv/lms

(89) Daniel A. Cox, 29th June 2021. Men's Social Circles are
Shrinking. Survey Center on American Life.
https://www.americansurveycenter.org/why-mens-social-
circles-are-shrinking/

(90) ONS Census 2021. 6th September 2022. Suicides in England and
Wales: 2021 registrations.
https://www.ons.gov.uk/peoplepopulationandcommunity/birth
sdeathsandmarriages/deaths/bulletins/suicidesintheunitedking
dom/2021registrations

(91) Bruce K. Alexander, Rat Park, 2010. Addiction: The View from
Rat Park. https://www.brucekalexander.com/articles-
speeches/rat-park/148-addiction-the-view-from-rat-park

(92) Daniel A. Cox, 8th June 2021. The State of American Friendship:
Change, Challenges, and Loss. Survey Center on American Life.
https://www.americansurveycenter.org/research/the-state-of-
american-friendship-change-challenges-and-loss/

(93) Ethnicity facts and figures, 3rd February 2023 (last updated 6th
July 2023). School teacher workforce. https://www.ethnicity-
facts-figures.service.gov.uk/workforce-and-
business/workforce-diversity/school-teacher-workforce/latest/

(94) Brad Wilcox, Wendy Wang, Alysse ElHage, 17th June 2022.
Institute of Family Studies. https://ifstudies.org/blog/life-

without-father-less-college-less-work-and-more-prison-for-young-men-growing-up-without-their-biological-father

(95) UK Parliament, Olympic Britain, Kid and kin. Children outside marriage. https://www.parliament.uk/business/publications/research/olympic-britain/housing-and-home-life/kid-and-kin/

(96) 1964, The Collected Works of Mahatma Gandhi, Volume XII, April 1913 to December 1914, Chapter: General Knowledge About Health XXXII: Accidents Snake-Bite, (From Gujarati, Indian Opinion, 9-8-1913), Start Page 156, Quote Page 158, The Publications Division, Ministry of Information and Broadcasting, Government of India. (Collected Works of Mahatma Ghandi at gandhiheritageportal.org.

(97) ONS, Census 2021. 2nd November 2022. 'Divorces in England and Wales: 2021'. https://www.ons.gov.uk/peoplepopulationandcommunity/birthsdeathsandmarriages/divorce/bulletins/divorcesinenglandandwales/2021

(98) Morgan Stanley, 23rd September 2019. 'Rise of the SHEconomy'. https://www.morganstanely.com/ideas/womens-impact-on-the-economy

(99) ONS, 27th January 2022 – Childbearing for women born in different years, England and Wales: 2020. https://www.ons.gov.uk/peoplepopulationandcommunity/birthsdeathsandmarriages/conceptionandfertilityrates/bulletins/childbearingforwomenbornindifferentyearsenglandandwales/2020/pdf

(100) Weisberg YJ, Deyoung CG, Hirsh JB. Gender Differences in Personality across the Ten Aspects of the Big Five. Front Psychol. 2011 Aug 1;2:178. doi: 10.3389/fpsyg.2011.00178. PMID: 21866227; PMCID: PMC3149680.

(101) Emily A. Vogels & Colleen McClain, 2nd February 2023. Key findings about online dating in the U.S. Pew Research Center. https://www.pewresearch.org/short-

reads/2023/02/02/key-findings-about-online-dating-in-the-u-s/.

(102)   @ChrisWillx, 12th November 2022 – (original source - The Joe Rogan Experience, 2nd August 2022. Podcast episode #1851 – Chris Williamson.
https://open.spotify.com/episode/3XMmLbHR7MUJsvrs3pmDWx Spotify)
https://x.com/ChrisWillx/status/1591491017680699392 X.

(103)   Jordan Peterson, 12 rules for life, rule 2 page 31.

(104)   Jimmy Carr, Before and Laughter page 178.

(105)   @petercrone, 6th March 2023.
https://www.instagram.com/p/CpdLdG7vbJb/ Instagram.

(106)   @consciousofficial_, Brian Cox (clip), 10th September 2023. https://www.instagram.com/reel/CxAcpN-NycK/ Instagram.

(107)   Modern Wisdom podcast, episode #383, 11th October 2021. Robert Greene – 12 Laws Of Power & Human Nature.
https://open.spotify.com/episode/2N185dueF9uT9MXaZ1bygh Spotify.

(108)   Modern Wisdom podcast, episode #721, 18th December 2023. George Mack – Why Can No One Think Rationally Anymore?
https://open.spotify.com/episode/1XdTjVHlKIqJNOjby6VUkC Spotify.

(109)   Jordan Peterson, 12 rules for life, rule 6 page 203.

(110)   The Gulag Archipelago 1918-1956, Aleksandr Solzhenitsyn.

(111)   @ChrisWillx 27th August 2023.
https://x.com/ChrisWillx/status/1695783230514069790 X.

(112)   John Shedd, Salt from My Attic.

(113)   The Joe Rogan Experience, 4th June 2019. Podcast episode #1309 – Naval Ravikant.
https://open.spotify.com/episode/3ijkVfaht5kcFPvHcCbYYD Spotify.

(114)   @IAmMarkManson, 11th March 2021.
https://x.com/IAmMarkManson/status/1264619673901060099
X.

(115)   Premier Unbelievable? 8th June 2018. Jordan Peterson
vs Susan Blackmore – Do we need God to make sense of life?
https://www.youtube.com/watch?v=syP-OtdClho YouTube.

(116)   Types of goal for sport rehabilitation (adapted from
Arvinen-Barrow and Hemmings, 2013, page 60).

(117)   Filby, W. C. D., Maynard, I. W., & Graydon, J. K. (1999).
The effect of multiple-goal strategies on performance
outcomes in training and competition. Journal of Applied Sport
Psychology, 11(2), 230–246.
https://doi.org/10.1080/10413209908404202.

(118)   James Clear, Atomic Habits page 27.

(119)   James Clear, Atomic Habits page 24.

(120)   James Clear, Atomic Habits page 24.

(121)   Kahneman D, Deaton A. High income improves
evaluation of life but not emotional well-being. Proc Natl Acad
Sci U S A. 2010 Sep 21;107(38):16489-93. doi:
10.1073/pnas.1011492107. Epub 2010 Sep 7. PMID: 20823223;
PMCID: PMC2944762.

(122)   @naval 24th March 2019.
https://x.com/naval/status/1109704032204009473 X / see also
'The Almanack of Naval Ravikant' by Eric Jorgenson, page 32.

(123)   Mischel W, Shoda Y, Rodriguez MI. Delay of
gratification in children. Science. 1989 May 26;244(4907):933-8.
doi: 10.1126/science.2658056. PMID: 2658056.

(124)   Wulfert E, Block JA, Santa Ana E, Rodriguez ML,
Colsman M. Delay of gratification: impulsive choices and
problem behaviors in early and late adolescence. J Pers. 2002
Aug;70(4):533-52. doi: 10.1111/1467-6494.05013. PMID:
12095190.

(125)   Mitchell SH. Measures of impulsivity in cigarette
smokers and non-smokers. Psychopharmacology (Berl). 1999
Oct;146(4):455-64. doi: 10.1007/pl00005491. PMID: 10550496.

(126)   @naval, 22nd February 2018.
https://x.com/naval/status/966512979066765313 X / see also
'The Almanack of Naval Ravikant' by Eric Jorgenson, page 124.

(127)   @RyanHoliday, 27th December 2021.
https://twitter.com/RyanHoliday/status/1475490912239341571
X.

(128)   @AlexHormozi, 6th August 2023.
https://x.com/AlexHormozi/status/1688189223021805568 X.

(129)   Gregory Matos PsyD. The Battle of the Sexes Has Left
More Couples Sexless. 7th October 2022. Psychology Today.
https://www.psychologytoday.com/intl/blog/the-state-our-unions/202210/the-battle-the-sexes-has-left-more-couples-sexless

(130)   Handelsman DJ, Hirschberg AL, Bermon S. Circulating
Testosterone as the Hormonal Basis of Sex Differences in
Athletic Performance. Endocr Rev. 2018 Oct 1;39(5):803-829.
doi: 10.1210/er.2018-00020. PMID: 30010735; PMCID:
PMC6391653.

(131)   The Joe Rogan Experience, 2nd August 2022. Podcast
episode #1851 – Chris Williamson.
https://open.spotify.com/episode/3XMmLbHR7MUJsvrs3pmD
Wx Spotify.

Printed in Great Britain
by Amazon